THE LAZARUS CHURCH

THE LAZARUS CHURCH

*Resurrecting Passionate Ministry
in Mainline Congregations*

JERRY MAYO

Providence House Publishers
PROVIDENCE PUBLISHING CORPORATION
FRANKLIN, TENNESSEE

Printed in the United States of America

08   07   06   05   04   1   2   3   4   5

Library of Congress Catalog Card Number: 2003112326

ISBN: 1-57736-292-6

Cover design by Matt McClane
Page design by John Tracy
Cover photo copyright © 2003, www.clipart.com

PROVIDENCE HOUSE PUBLISHERS
an imprint of
Providence Publishing Corporation
238 Seaboard Lane • Franklin, Tennessee 37067
www.providence-publishing.com
800-321-5692

To Patricia,
with love and gratitude.

and

To Amos White Mayo (1922–2001),
who was never heard to say, "I'm tired!"

CONTENTS

INTRODUCTION

IN A TIME WHEN OTHER RELIGIOUS GROUPS ARE rapidly growing their membership and expanding their global influence, why is it that the mainline Christian church seems to be dwindling? One reason could be that we are sometimes fuzzy in our witness to the central truths of the faith. People aren't sure what we are asking them to believe. When the world hears the voices of the old churches denying the centrality of Christ, disputing the primacy of Scripture, and disavowing the power of God's grace in Christ, then what conclusion can the world draw about the church?

The need for renewal in mainline Christian denominations is urgent. Raw statistics alone paint a dismal picture. From 1965 through 1999, the

Episcopal, Presbyterian (U.S.A.), and United Methodist churches lost a total of 4,638,000 adherents. These churches claimed 18,343,000 members in 1965, yet in 1999 they only had 13,605,000 members—they lost more than a quarter of their membership over a period of 34 years. If this rate of loss were to continue, then in less than 150 years (fewer than the years they have existed) they would cease to exist. It appears that this pattern of loss has continued, and in some cases, accelerated since 1999. Too few leaders and members of local congregations seem concerned by this ominous reality, yet the story of all mainline churches is not much different than the record of these three. If we believe the historic witness of these churches is valuable, then it is urgent that they find a renewed passion for Christ.

St. Paul calls us to reclaim the historical, ecumenical, and universal church's clear and compelling message. First, we are reminded that, "Even in the case of lifeless things that make sounds, such as the flute or harp, how will anyone know what tune is being played unless there is a distinction in the notes? Again, if the trumpet does not sound a clear call, who will get ready for battle?" (1 Cor. 14:7–8). Also, "And if Christ has not been raised, our preaching is useless and so is your faith" (1 Cor. 15:14). To raise these old churches to new life, there must be a rediscovery of the core values, central convictions, and classic theology of the church.

The important issue of the inclusive love of Christ is often politicized. I was recently the guest on a radio talk show where the host asked me if I thought American society had paid too much attention to political correctness. My response was surprising to him and to me—I found myself saying that if it is a matter of loving and caring for people who are excluded by language and social structures, then political correctness is a good and right thing. However, when it is manipulated for personal power to the degree that we lose sight of our responsibility to lift up life and bless people, then it is wrong and destructive. Sometimes, a desire for political correctness has fueled the leadership of the old churches to the point that they seem more like activist groups than agents of the redemptive grace of Jesus Christ. This is at least the perception of many inside and outside these churches.

These few realities and many others call the churches to turn once again to Jesus Christ as He is known in changed hearts and lives, witnessed to in history, and declared in Holy Scripture. The churches need to experience and proclaim Jesus Christ as the creative, redeeming power of God. Only in this manner can old churches that seem to be destined for death be raised to powerful new life and witness in the world.

Although I am now pastor of a large and rapidly growing congregation, I began my ministry on a four-church charge. I have served a 10-member congregation and enjoyed it. I can testify to the fact that this hope, God's incredible resurrection power, is available to all congregations regardless of size. My most memorable evangelism program was at the Fountain Grove Church on the Hickory Creek Circuit, my first appointment as a twenty-one-year-old student pastor. This little one-room church that sat on stacked rocks was located in the country near the spring-fed Hickory Creek and was nestled among large oak trees. While I was there, a member of the congregation asked me to preach a revival. I had no supply of sermons, so I told him that they had already heard all of my messages. To my surprise, he said it didn't matter, that I could preach them again. Here was a good group of people who wanted to confirm a young minister's call, although they would not have used such theological and technical terms. They just wanted to help me have a good beginning. The congregation worked hard planning meals and inviting people to the revival. They shared their faith and gave their own witness. At the close of the week there were nineteen people who had professed their faith and who were baptized the following Sunday afternoon in Hickory Creek. I learned in Fountain Grove that any congregation can be vital when people care and act unselfishly to reach out to others with the love of Christ.

I have served many positions of leadership in the church, from chairing District and Conference Boards of Ordained Ministry, to being coordinator of District Youth Work, to making mission trips, to serving as a district superintendent, to being a delegate to four General Conferences of my denomination. Yet my roots are in the small church that struggles to have enough resources and people to attempt to embrace its Christian mission. I know that the power of Christ is most experienced in the local church where God's love is obviously present.

Any congregation can be vital
when people care and act unselfishly
to reach out to others with the love of Christ.

Any church can become a Lazarus church raised to new life in the Lord. Any pastor can become a Lazarus leader of a vital congregation. Early in my ministry I learned the promise of Christ, "My grace is sufficient for you, for my power is made perfect in weakness" (2 Cor. 12:9 NIV). Until we believe this truth, we cannot risk what it takes to raise up Lazarus churches. I am just an ordinary pastor who hopes to hold onto this truth and find a way to live into its power. This book is my prayer on behalf of the mainline churches and an appeal to our people to recognize the imperative of seeking the life-restoring power of Christ for our beloved churches.

THE LAZARUS
CHURCH

Chapter One

LAZARUS PRINCIPLES FOR THE CHURCH

GOD SEEMS TO HAVE DRAWN ME TO THE LAZARUS story in the gospel of John as the vehicle by which to affirm my love and hope for the church. You are probably familiar with this story, but if you read it with fresh eyes as I did, there are many lessons for the church to be discovered in these verses. I encourage you to lift it up as a story of hope for the church and glean from it the principles of new life.

Lazarus is sick. His sisters Mary and Martha send word to Jesus: "Lord, the one you love is sick" (John 11:3). But Jesus delays His coming because He has other tasks to attend. A few days later, Jesus tells His disciples He is going back to Judea. The disciples remind Him that the people of Judea tried to kill Him and that He should not go there. Jesus tells them, "Our friend Lazarus has fallen asleep; but I am going there to wake him up" (John 11:11). The disciples do not realize that Lazarus is dead until Jesus puts it bluntly: "Lazarus is dead" (John 11:14). Jesus tells them He is glad He was not there to prevent the death so that they might see and believe.

When Jesus arrives at Bethany he discovers that Lazarus has been dead for four days. Martha goes out first to meet Jesus and declares that if Jesus had been present, Lazarus would not have died. Jesus states that her brother will rise again, but Martha cannot believe it. Jesus tells her that He is the resurrection and life, and whoever believes in Him will never really die. Jesus asks her if she believes this. The moment of confessed faith comes when Martha says, "Yes, Lord, I believe that you are the Messiah, the Son of God, the one coming into the world" (John 11:27).

Mary goes out to meet Jesus when Martha returns home. The professional mourners go with her, flailing their arms, tearing their clothes, throwing dust in the air, and catching their tears in little bottles. When Mary meets Jesus, she makes the same accusation that Martha made when she met Jesus: had Jesus come sooner, her brother would not have died.

Jesus is so deeply moved by Mary's tears and grief and by the power of His own love for Lazarus that He simply weeps. The people present are touched by how much Jesus loves Lazarus.

Jesus asks them to take away the tombstone. Everyone thinks Jesus is foolish, since Lazarus is stinking dead. Then Jesus declares that He told them they would see the glory of God. He prays not because it is necessary, but so the people will know by whose power what is about to happen will occur and believe He was sent by God.

Jesus calls Lazarus out of the tomb and asks the people to take off his death wrappings and let him go. Many people witness Lazarus's resurrection and tell others, and quite a stir erupts. Some who observe the miracle of new life believe in Jesus because of Lazarus.

Jesus leaves Bethany and then returns later—six days before Passover. Bethany is now referred to as the place where Lazarus lived, not where he was buried. A great feast ensues. Lazarus is at the table with Jesus in this feast of life with his family and neighbors.

LAZARUS PRINCIPLES FOR THE CHURCH

The first Lazarus principle is that *the church is loved.* Jesus comes with restorative power for Lazarus; it is Jesus' love for Lazarus that brings him to Bethany. In a similar way, Jesus loves the church—the old main-line church, too—and brings to it His power for new life. After all, Jesus established the church—it is life of His life, the body of Christ. Just as Mary and Martha loved Lazarus, the Marys and Marthas of the church family are members who love their church and serve it with care. The church's hope is in the love power of Christ and His people, those who love the church love Him and are loved by Him.

The second Lazarus principle is that *the church needs Jesus.* The church is sometimes sick. Often it sleeps. On occasion it is dead, entombed in troubles and weaknesses that rob it of life. When the church loses its focus on Jesus, it is separated from its life power. The church's hope to live vitally is found in Jesus Christ. He is as much the Savior of the church as He is of the world. Just as Lazarus's life hope was found only in the arrival of Jesus, so the church's true life is released when Jesus arrives.

It is through the Holy Scripture and through prayer that we come into the presence of Jesus who raises the church and us to new life. In the Old Testament the formation and reformation of the people of God are associated with discovery of God's Word—God speaks and life is birthed. Israel is guided and sustained by the prayers of Moses and shaped by the Word God gave Moses on the mountain. The joy of David and the people overflowed when the Ark of the Covenant was brought into Jerusalem and that city was made the spiritual center of the land. The Word was at the center of this golden age of Israel's history. Josiah's reform of Judah in an evil age was inspired by the discovery of the Book of the Law, which had been lost and forgotten. When the people returned from Babylonian exile and the wall was first completed, the people assembled before the Water

Gate and asked Ezra to bring out the Book of the Law. He stood on a high wooden platform and, as the Book of the Law was unrolled, the people stood up and a great spiritual renewal was experienced.

So too, all great revivals of the church have at their center renewed interest in Bible reading and study and in prayer. We open our lives to encounter the Christ—Jesus of Nazareth—when the Holy Spirit speaks to us from God's Word and when in prayer the Holy Spirit brings into our lives a Jesus consciousness. Lazarus is awakened when Jesus comes calling in response to prayer—the pleas and requests and messages sent by Mary and Martha to Jesus.

My congregation, First United Methodist Church of Murfreesboro, Tennessee, which had worshipped in its old sanctuary since 1888, recently moved into a new facility. We made our journey by a strong focus on Holy Scriptures and on the wings of prayer. On the Saturday afternoon before our first Sunday services in the new building, our procession into the new sanctuary was led by our Ark of the Covenant—the pulpit and the Bible. The Word was placed on the altar, and we will gather our life of faith around this Word that has sustained us in our history. We prayed our way into this new place. During construction we gathered regularly for prayer walks around the new facilities and stopped at designated stations where Bible verses and thousands of white prayer ribbons were tied to the construction fence. God spoke to us in the Word and in prayer. Jesus became the focus of our move. We are still becoming a Lazarus church by Scripture and by prayer—in this manner God brings Jesus into our church.

The third Lazarus principle is that *the church must place its faith in the resurrection power of Jesus to bring new life.* When Mary and Martha sent for Jesus they invited a great power—they became partners with Him when they confessed, ". . . you are the Messiah, the Son of God, the one coming into the world" (John 11:27). In order to unleash Jesus' life-restoring power, the Lazarus church must profess and proclaim this faith.

The fourth Lazarus principle is that *the church lives most joyfully when it is at the table with Jesus and gives its witness to Jesus' life power.* The joy of the church is felt most deeply when it takes the bread and cup of Jesus' life given in death for it. When at this table of grace, the church experiences the risen Lord within. In the Lazarus story, the joyful celebration of new life and Jesus' resurrection power takes place at a family meal to which neighbors and friends are all invited. Likewise, Lazarus's greatest joy was found when his new life drew others to that table of fellowship—this is the shared feast of the inbreaking kingdom of God. The Lazarus church must welcome people to God's table to sup with them.

The fifth Lazarus principle is that *it is the awakening and resurrecting life given by Jesus which leads the* church to the dangerous place of being perceived as a threat to the world; yet the life it has received and witnesses to is the hope of the world. The Lazarus church and its people become a sacramental offering and suffer as signs of grace—misunderstood and threatened by life in the world, yet exuding the "Jesus life" given to them. In the Lazarus story the leaders who were threatened by Jesus' ministry plotted to kill both Jesus and Lazarus. There is danger in coming alive in Jesus Christ. The mainline churches must discover a radical faith in Jesus and a strong witness to the resurrected life to be found in Him even at the risk of being misunderstood. Life involves risk and conflict. Lazarus churches will take this risk.

The Lazarus church is the church that experiences and knows the power of the Lazarus principles, and it is only made alive by Christ. It is a church powerful in attraction—bringing many into Christ's outreaching love. Such a church is vital in the mercy of the Lord. It can be small or large, poor or rich, housed in a great cathedral or in a storefront. It is Jesus who makes the Lazarus church sing and soar and live the life of victorious grace.

My greatest prayer is that all churches would become true Lazarus churches. If I can share this concept alone, then this book will be a seed well planted. I ask God's grace for this book and for the churches and the people who read and study it.

Chapter Two

HOPE FOR THE TWENTY-FIRST CENTURY CHURCH

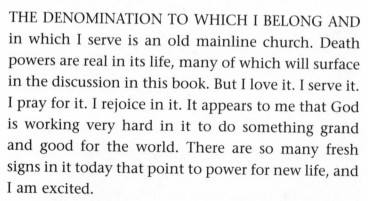

THE DENOMINATION TO WHICH I BELONG AND in which I serve is an old mainline church. Death powers are real in its life, many of which will surface in the discussion in this book. But I love it. I serve it. I pray for it. I rejoice in it. It appears to me that God is working very hard in it to do something grand and good for the world. There are so many fresh signs in it today that point to power for new life, and I am excited.

I believe that the old mainline churches can be Lazarus churches, full of hope that Jesus who raised Lazarus can raise them also to new life. I am gripped by this simple thought: *Jesus alone must save His church.* Christ must be offered in a new way not only to the world, but to the church itself. If we can get

Jesus to Lazarus, then Lazarus can rise to new and passionate life.

So many good people in so many of the old mainline congregations love their churches and try to stir them into life. I wonder how the old traditional churches can find such new wineskins for the ancient, universal, and enduring gospel expressions so unique to their history and so needed in our time and in the future. Can old churches find humility to learn from people like Michael Slaughter who talks about "unlearning church" in his book by that title?[1] His many wonderful stories of how numerous congregations have found new vitality should capture the minds of the leaders of the old churches.

The postmodern time in which we live is awakening many hearts to God's potential. Leonard Sweet's appeal for the church to have a first-century passion for the twenty-first century world is a wonderful call to new life. His description of an "EPIC" church in which worship and congregational life is experiential, participatory, image-driven, and connected is worthy of pondering and acting on.[2] In his book *Blueprint 21*, Robert Thornton Henderson finds the Presbyterian church's connectionalism to be a focus for hope and identity. He writes, "For all our vaunted connectionalism, it is only our theological consensus and our missional consensus which are the glue that give us coherence. It is these that give us our integrity in our calling to be about the *Missio Dei*, the mission of God.

If there is no consensus on these, then there is nothing that connects us."3

In his book *Churchquake*, Peter Wagner speaks of God shaking things up and calls the churches to find ways to embrace the renewed interest in and expression of the worship of God in this time.4 Richard Kew and Bishop Roger White have dared to call for a radical new reformation of the Episcopal church. They thread throughout their book two beliefs. First, "the environment in which we are called to be the church is changing rapidly and radically, and . . . we ignore this reality at our peril." Secondly, "the organizing principle of tomorrow's church must be the business of mission, witness, and evangelism."5

When we set such thoughts as these alongside the classical expressions of faith and yoke them to the biblical witness for clarity and direction, we can begin to discern how they serve the purposes of Jesus Christ. Then we have the powerful potential for bringing to new life great and powerful Lazarus churches. There are many reasons why old mains should be resurrected, and a few stand out in my mind.

THE ORIGINS AND DIVERSITY OF OLD MAINS

The old mainline churches emerged from the powers of renewal birthed in history by the Spirit of God. They once were young and new on the church scene. They arose out of the longing of human hearts for a personal spiritual awakening and the response of "Jesus-shaped" lives to human pain and need. The great Protestant Reformation, the Anabaptists, Calvinism, the Wesleyan Revival, the Great Awakening, and the camp meetings of the Holiness movement in our country are examples of the origin of these old mainline churches.

Will we greet the current age with ministry, worship, and mission that connect with people and embrace them with an ageless truth?

In the past the old churches emerged to meet the new generation by communicating the gospel in a way that spoke directly to people's lives. Martin Luther's proclamation of salvation by grace and the place of faith launched the Protestant Reformation of the sixteenth century. John and Charles Wesley went into streets, mines, homes, and prisons with a word that matched the age in which they lived. They wrote new hymns using psalms set to bar tunes that the common people could understand. The question today is, will the old mainline churches of the Protestant movement meet the people of this generation with an experience of the faith that has meaning for their personal lives? Will we greet the current age with ministry, worship, and mission that connect with people and embrace them with an ageless truth?

Will the old churches be willing to reach back into their own history and risk themselves in the hands of this global twenty-first century culture? The answer to this question will determine the ultimate success of the church.

The old mainline churches have been where the new and emerging churches are today. They have created new hymnody and flung off old wineskins only to return to them and their enduring meaning. These once-young churches, now old in the eyes of the world, must learn how to rediscover the value and truth of God's grace—the life of Jesus—in high sacramental expression through baptismal and liturgical renewal around the table of the Lord. Indeed, the old churches have made mistakes, but many have found innovative ways to spread the gospel to new generations, and have learned how to make the eternal words of the Bible real to young minds.

At their hearts, mainline churches know a lot about being reborn. They may have stood for over two hundred years and survived successive changes in the culture of generations, yet again, they had to be created anew for every successive generation or they would have ceased existing. The old churches often are to the new churches what our parents are to us: as we grow older we know our parents have much to give us, yet we often reject their wisdom. When our parents die and we find ourselves without them, we wish we could just ask them their thoughts and listen to them. Mothers and fathers often wish for some way to impart the lessons learned and expressed in traditions proven and true.

---

*If it were not for
the old mainline churches
who kept the Jesus story and the sacraments
for succeeding generations,
there would be no Christianity
for the new churches to preach or share.*

Many questions must be answered if the old churches are to become Lazarus churches. Why is it so difficult for us to learn from the immediate past generation, and why is it so difficult for one generation to pass along the truths it has learned to the next generation? Will the group that has held onto the powerful traditions of the church seek to incorporate the emerging generation's expressions of faith? Can it release the gospel power of prayer and Scripture into the hands of those newly discovering it? Or will this generation hold onto it with impunity? What is the responsibility of parents of the faith to the children?

If it were not for the old mainline churches who kept the Jesus story and the sacraments for succeeding generations, there would be no Christianity for the new churches to preach or share. If all at once we could expunge from history the old mainline churches—all their institutions such as colleges, universities, hospitals, and missions—and if all the lives they touched were never touched by them, our world would be a place void of many values, millions would have died without the touch of eternal grace, and our world would be much more hell-like than it is. If we erased the great art and literature inspired by the old churches, our world would be less able to aspire to the heights of the soul. If we removed the soul-stirring music that the old churches created, we would be trapped in surface expressions of the heart.

We need the ancient witness of these churches reborn in song and melody that reaches into the deep places of our being. It is noteworthy that when a national crisis comes, America and its churches turn not to praise choruses or songs, but to the great hymns such as "O God our Help in Ages Past" and "A Mighty Fortress Is Our God." There is a lesson to be learned about an unchanging God in times and tunes like these. Maybe contemporary worship needs wedding to the old texts and tunes to form "a mighty fortress" against the despairs and fears of the new century. Could the old be resurrected in the new with abiding witness to the dependable nature and faithfulness of God? Could the essentials of the old churches be the real vitality of the new expressions? Maybe we are family and not enemies.

In many ways we, today's Christians, owe everything to these old churches. We should value and bless them. We should heed the admonition, "Honor thy father and thy mother." In their origins old mains are pure and powerful, born of the power from above in unique and diverse expressions, yet filled with every expression of human sin that is part of any spiritual movement. God is hard to put in a box, and God's church is hard to keep in the tomb.

The churches from which our old mainlines were spawned, while suffering the labor pains of delivering new churches now old, found renewal and sustaining powers of life themselves. The power with which they remain with us speaks of the life Lazarus churches can discover across the centuries in an abiding witness and ministry. The needs out of which the old mains were born are still present for the ministry of these churches to embrace and meet.

If old mains can find a passionate power for the gospel of Christ and for the people of the world, then the diversity represented in them is needed in a very diverse age. Not everyone is looking for or reached by one form of worship or by one kind of religious expression. Old churches, if allowed to claim their classic faith and recapture their passion, know who they are because of their long history of thinking, praying, worshipping, and serving. Their sense of identity, if reclaimed and renewed, makes it possible for them to accept people who want an honest search without having to pretend to have it all put together or without having had an experience that makes honest searching unnecessary. These old churches can be safe places for people looking for God and waiting upon Christ that are unique in our loud and thrashing world.

There is indeed some worth in the origin and diversity of the old mainline churches that warrants rolling back the stones and unbinding them. Jesus knows this and is ready to join us in this ministry to revive the churches.

THE VALUE OF THE OLD MAINS' PRESENT WITNESS

In our ever-changing world, where so little is certain, people have trouble finding anything to which they can anchor their lives. Are there any unchanging realities that are predictable and secure?

Because of their longevity and enduring life, mainline churches hold within them the possibility of witnessing to a Christ who is the same yesterday, today, and tomorrow. The author of Hebrews writes about the need to hang onto this central truth that has the power to hold us. "Jesus Christ is the same yesterday and today and forever. Do not be carried away by all kinds of teachings. It is good for our hearts to be strengthened by grace . . ." (Heb. 13:8–9).

Old churches have a practice of religion that bears witness to the truth that God is the same. The core of their worship reflects the synagogue worship of Judaism, adopted by the early church and shaped over two thousand years of history. This worship has worked for a long time in the old churches' witness to a God who does not change and on whom we can depend. Although old churches offer variety in forms of worship, they hold at the center an expression of word, song, prayer, sacrament, and community that has worked for a long time.

In the midst of worship wars and changing styles, we now find a generation of people who want order and seek liturgy that works. The liturgy of the old churches, when breathed with new warmth and excitement, can perhaps be the best vehicle of such worship and at the same time remind us that Christ is eternally the same. Ritual breathed with life offers exciting participation for everyone through common words, movement, and community sharing. The sanctuaries of the old traditions can certainly meet the need for visual images with the beauty of stained glass windows depicting age-old stories, the visual presence and powerful sound of a pipe organ unleashed, and the pomp of processionals and banners. Ritual of ancient origin filled with fresh spirit breath can be a glorious expression of faith in significant pageantry and imagery. Sharing ritual with others gives belonging—connection. Instead of the focus in worship being a personality up front, the focus is on God unseen, the work of the community of faith in worship, and the place of the individual in God's community. The focus is shifted away from a leader onto the order of worship that lifts the people together into the presence of the Holy Spirit. One of the more remarkable worship services I have attended was at an old main church. I truly worshipped. Leaving the parking lot after the service, it dawned on me that I hardly noticed the ministers at the altar. They were not obvious. *God* was obvious. Old churches with ancient ways can be the instrument of divine grace in worship that focuses on Christ, not the people leading the service.

Old mains must not be so rigid
as to cause their own people to have to go outside
their church to experience the Holy Spirit.

Mainline churches must enliven and reshape traditional worship to meet the needs of the emerging generation. Contemporary worship would benefit from the church's ancient witness and discipline. There is a real need for the inclusion of varieties of worship experiences in our diverse world. Many sincere people in our congregations love traditional worship yet also long for a contemporary worship experience in their own church. Old mains must not be so rigid as to cause their own people to have to go outside their church to experience the Holy Spirit. To deny their people this kind of opportunity is to deny their own history.

The new dynamics of worship and the interest in it that creates debate and sometimes conflict are a sign of hope. I recently participated in a conference at a very large church that has been on the cutting edge of growth for thirty years. The minister of music spoke of worship wars and that, after all these years, churches are now faced with the emerging truth that the young generation wants liturgy. A minister friend of mine whose work has been focused on contemporary praise and worship spoke with me recently. His research and reading are now telling him that the next wave of growth is going to require form, order, and ritual in worship.

Is there a craving hunger in the human heart for God who is dependable, and for enduring expressions of God that are central to the ministries of the older churches? Is the message that God is the same deeply needed? I believe so. Albert Edward Day confirms that belief with these comforting words:

When we say that God is holy, we are not naming an attribute among many others such as love and mercy and wisdom and power. We are attempting to designate something that applies to all his attributes, something that gives them an awesome dimension. We are saying that he is the changeless One. His love never fluctuates; his mercy is inexhaustible; his wisdom cherishes all that is truly good; his power can always be trusted to act redemptively. The supreme wonder and unrivalled glory is that he is all that he is, unchangeably.[6]

Are old mainline churches uniquely equipped to speak this message in form and even in architecture through which God's light speaks in brilliant colors?

What will the Lazarus church be to this changing world? Can old mains and our own congregations be true Lazarus churches raised up and set free?

OLD MAINS ARE CHURCHES WITH RESURRECTION POTENTIAL

The potential of the old mainline churches is phenomenal. Mainline churches have a franchise on millions of lives that demand their awakening into new vitality. These millions look to their traditions for faith and witness. What will happen to these people if the mainline church fails them? We have no choice but to tend to the awakening of the old mainline churches.

In his book *The Index of Leading Spiritual Indicators*, George Barna provides some information that speaks of the resurrection potential of the old mainline churches. His studies indicate that, "Most adults have moderately favorable attitudes toward the major denominational groups in the U.S.A. A majority hold favorable impressions of Baptist churches (65 percent either very favorable or somewhat favorable impressions), Methodist churches (60 percent). . . . Half maintain a favorable view of Presbyterian Churches (50 percent) . . . Lutheran churches (47 percent)."[7] It is imperative that the old mainline churches be found alive and passionate about all these people and aggressively offer the love of Christ to these millions.

Old mainline churches are part of the holy universal and ecumenical expression of the body of Christ, the church of the Lord. They hold within them great talent, highly educated as well as uneducated people, poor and rich, and many resources for service to Christ. They are uniquely gifted to be a powerhouse for God by their history, the people in them today, and their worldwide connections that new and independent churches do not always have available to them. Old mainline churches have at their core the knowledge of Jesus, the promises of Jesus, and the expectation of Jesus. They are churches with resurrection potential. They now encounter the power and possibility of being enlivened by Jesus Himself.

This truth compels me to write this book, not because I am wise or insightful, or that my words carry any authority, or because any recognition of my name might cause someone to read them—for none of this is true. I write this book because I believe in the power available to the church I love, and I believe the old mainline churches have locked up in them a value the world desperately needs. I want the old churches to believe in their value and the power of Jesus' life within them.

Chapter Three

THE DIVORCED CHURCH

THE STORY OF LAZARUS DEPICTS THE DESPAIR, anger, and confusion that exists in those whose lives have been centered on Jesus after a distance grows between them and the Lord. When Jesus is absent from the scene, hopelessness prevails, and there is no victorious power of life to confront the powers of death. When Jesus is not the central presence of its life and the Holy Spirit is absent, the church is caught up in all kinds of expressions of powerlessness.

The absence of Jesus as the focus of the church is similar to people who live only in their heads—by their intellect alone and not by their heart power.

24

Such a church seeks comfort in people who lack vision. People get confused about why the church exists, and begin to view it as a spiritual supermarket—if it can only offer enough programs, then consumers of religion will come and sample its products. If the church is seen as a place where people buy services with their giving, then tears and anger prevail when the church does not provide products to satisfy its customers.

Services received instead of servanthood lived out can hinder the mission and witness of the church in people's lives. A member of a congregation I served as pastor was hospitalized. She lived alone and her children all lived out of state. She was a precious servant of Christ who had given much to the church. In recent years she had become semi-shut-in, so she was assigned a special visitor from the membership of the church who visited her weekly. The minister of congregational care went by regularly, and the *Upper Room* devotion was delivered to her by hand every two months. Special friends from her Sunday school class contacted her frequently. Yet, because she had some mild dementia, she did not understand that all this care was from her church, so she felt the church was not reaching out to her. Her children who were not nearby to observe the care of the congregation were disappointed in their perceived failure of the church. As is always the case, I am sure the church could

have done more and better than it had done. The
family contacted the church in anger, and they
referred to how they sent contributions to the
church and that the church should be doing better
by their mother. I understood their anger and knew
some of it was their own frustration at not being
able to be present with their mother more and their
wish that the congregation could replace their own
sensed need to be more available to their mother. I
knew they loved her dearly and were doing the best
they could for her and showed their care greatly and
in a good manner. The thing that stood out to me
was that they felt they had paid the church to take
care of their mother—that they had purchased its
services and they were dissatisfied customers.

> *To find the liberation of servanthood*
> *and the joy of being an offering of Jesus' love*
> *and a gift of grace to life*
> *is a freedom that cannot be surpassed.*

All pastors have had to deal with some individuals
who believed they gave enough to the church to be
treated differently than other members. Sometimes
a church and its people can fall into believing, in
practice, that the members who have the most
money and are able to give more have purchased
more services of the church than other members
who do not have as much money and cannot give as

much. The whole doctrine of grace—the mercy of Jesus Christ—gets lost in such consumerist religion. We forget that the church not only ministers to us, but that we are called into the church to be ministers of Christ ourselves. To find the liberation of servanthood and the joy of being an offering of Jesus' love and a gift of grace to life is a freedom that cannot be surpassed.

How we speak of the reasons we chose a particular church to join is very revealing. We talk about the products developed for public consumption. We choose to join because of what the church offers our family and us in terms of programs and facilities. Sometimes a few of us join a particular church because we are needed there, because this is the place we feel we can best serve Christ, or because we feel the power of God's call on our lives, or because in this church we felt we truly worshipped God and were free to give ourselves to God in Christ there. Discipleship has in it Jesus' call to take up our crosses, deny ourselves, and follow Him. The fact that we miss this message so central to being raised to life in Jesus is very revealing. This may unveil the core problems of many of our churches. The heart of the Christian faith is discipleship—loving, serving, and following Jesus in giving our lives as an offering to God. We can miss the heart of the church's faith so easily in a consumer-minded world.

Churches that are made up primarily of consumers of religion who do not know the life of Christ have a hard time helping people become disciples of Jesus. The members of consumer churches are frustrated by the absence of something they cannot define and sometimes begin to think the church is to be their family chapel and that the pastor is to be their private chaplain. Consumer churches are bound up in their own grief, and they miss the joy of seeing and experiencing the church as an offering of their lives to the great God of all creation and of being received by God through Jesus. These churches are divorced from their God-given purpose to make it possible for people to be encountered by God and to experience abundant life in Jesus Christ—to become lives lived in Christ as gifts of joy.

In the early part of the story of Lazarus we meet Mary and Martha and those trying to console them, a scene much like that which often prevails in the church. Remember that Jesus loves the church and the members love it, too. Yet there is a void that separates the church and its people from God's intentions. Lazarus is described as being loved by his sisters, Mary and Martha, and the Lord Jesus, too. Yet none of this was enough to keep Lazarus alive and there was no hope for him as long as Jesus was absent.

Mary and Martha were angry with the Lord, frustrated with one another, and irritated by the people around them. Something vital was missing. It was Jesus. Mary and Martha both seemed to accuse Jesus with angry words when they both said: "If you had been here, [our] brother would not have died" (John 11:21,32). Jesus replied, "Your brother will rise again" (John 11:23). Martha responds in such a manner that she seems to be saying, "Sure, when it doesn't matter any more, when life is over and the dead are raised." Some of us have about as much hope for the church as Mary and Martha did for Lazarus.

What Jesus wants Martha to know is that He is the resurrection and the life. He is the heart of her hope and of Lazarus's hope. Until she could know this and live into its truth, she would not know her own heart's hope. Jesus says to Martha what Jesus says to the church, "I am the resurrection and the life. . . . Do you believe this?" (John 11:25–26). Everything hangs on the answer to this question.

Jesus wept by the tomb of Lazarus who was dead, and for Mary and Martha's lack of faith in Him. Jesus weeps for the sleeping church and the death shadows enshrouding it. Like Mary and Martha, the people of the church can be divorced from the heart of hope and life in Christ that will empower them.

THE DIVORCED CHURCH

Many people have lost their expectation for a good life because of the decline of the stable and loving family environment where people are bound together in mutual affection, where faithfulness and dependability characterize life. Pessimism about the future may, among many other things, be rooted in the experience of broken relationships that once could have been a source of security and predictability.

The church is affected by the character and health of the homes of its people. When hearts are broken and alienated from one another in our most basic relationships, the church loses much of its power and resourcefulness for ministry and mission. When people feel no one loves them, they lack a passion for living and their lives are filled with negative emotions. These negative emotions spill out in behaviors that further shatter life—eating disorders, drug addictions, lust, sleep disorders, addiction to pornography, workaholism, loss of energy, impatience, and controlling behaviors—these and multitudes of other symptoms reveal hearts with unmet needs. People hunger for fellowship with someone who will understand and appreciate them, stand by them, and love them.

People who feel disconnected from others who value them need the power of a church that is alive with hope. Of all the places they go, they should find within the church a heart of love and grace that abounds with the anticipation that with God, goodness is still available for all people. How difficult it is to enliven people who come to the church seeking comfort and restoration when the church itself is hopeless, filled with despair, and fearful for its own survival. A defeated church cannot offer encouragement to others. The victorious, powerful, resurrected Jesus—who transcends our powerlessness with unending love and the promise of fulfillment—is the power of the church's witness. The risen Christ is the power that holds the church in hope so that it can lift up the stooped shoulders of the people who finally get up enough courage to enter its doors.

We who are in the church must dare
to become so vulnerable to our own suffering
and to the suffering of the world
as to find that God is able
to sustain us in hope.

The church must find its own heart in order to enliven the hearts of others. Jesus is the heart of God—the love power of God—that provides the church, the body of Christ, with its true heart.

We who are in the church must dare to become so vulnerable to our own suffering and to the suffering of the world as to find that God is able to sustain us in hope. A church that casts itself unselfishly into the arms of God and places itself in the guiding, sustaining hands of Jesus becomes vulnerable enough to find hope and to make this hope a gift to others.

However, we can so shelter ourselves from the pain and demands of life, from the needs of others, and from the call to be vulnerable and accessible to God that we lose touch with our own healthy feelings. We can intellectualize life experiences until we have no idea that within us there could be an untapped reservoir of ardent love, of abundant and glad joy, or a potential explosion of enthusiasm for living.

I recall with grief and joy discovering my own lost feelings. During a particularly painful time in my life, two special people to whom I was very close were victimized by alcohol and drug addiction. They were both beautiful people of amazing potential. They were sensitive and caring, qualities which perhaps made them more vulnerable to the terrors of drugs and alcohol. Peer pressure, consciousness of life's unfairness, and a thousand unnamed things cracked open a door in their lives and allowed these demons to enter. I suddenly faced a power over which I had no control. I felt helpless, like I was a failure in my love for them. I was filled with shame and embarrassment. Instead of being driven only by my love and concern for them, the evil of self-concern grabbed my heart and I acted out my fear in angry words and strange manners. Something had to be done. Pressures bore down upon me, and I wanted to hide. I felt alienated, like what I had imagined my life to be was only a fantasy created in my mind.

At times I felt as if I could not go on in ministry, that I had given all I could give and that it was not enough. I missed the easy relationship with Jesus that I had taken for granted. I felt a separation from life, and I didn't want anyone to know about it. I was a preacher, and this kind of thing just didn't happen to preachers—shame! I had replaced my focus on Christ in my life and in my church with ideals of what Christian people and the Christian church are supposed to be, and these ideals did not include suffering, powerlessness, or recognition of a sense of failure. I saw things I did not like in myself—qualities I abhorred and never imagined would be part of me. I was up against something I could not overcome, and I felt overwhelmed and distraught.

My loved ones eventually sought help that I could not give. Then I made myself available for counseling with them, which meant I had to become vulnerable and accessible—stop hiding and pretending. The counselor asked me to tell her how I felt, and I started talking rather freely. She stopped me and said, "No, don't tell me what you think. Tell me how you feel." This happened several times. Finally, I broke down and wept. I did not know how I felt—I had lost touch with my own heart. Now I know exactly how I felt, but this came only after Jesus became more obviously present in all the strange gifts of grace that little by little I began to see. I discovered that my thorns had roses.

I did not realize how being divorced from my own heart had affected my relationship with others and with God. This divorce had infiltrated the very spirit, or the lack thereof, of my faith and ministry. I felt like a lifeless preacher in a lifeless church.

As I acknowledged my neediness, a change began to occur until God's heart met my heart with a love that was full of feeling, overpowering truth, and reality. In my growing awareness of God's feelings for me (revealed in Jesus' near presence), I was free to know my own heart for the first time. In inspired moments of prayer God gradually and gently led me back into fullness of life where I was energized. Spirituality grew and new enthusiasm for ministry exploded all over me.

I am not a very outward person, but I am straightforward. This heart discovery may not manifest itself in the way some people would expect it. Yet, in my heart, in keeping with the temperament of my character, grows a new fire. After thirty-six years of ministry I am more excited and hopeful today than ever before. Now I feel like a Lazarus preacher serving a Lazarus church that is waking each day to new life—although greatly challenged and challenging.

Being saved from despair and discovering renewal for ministry is a matter of reconciliation of hearts— God's and ours—and of our hearts with the hearts of the people God has placed in our lives. I rejoice in the new life of Jesus present in my life and the happiness of two people I love being closer to me now than ever before. I enjoy seeing them free and joined in life with others who love them. I wish and pray that this could be so for everyone who faces such demons and separation from his or her true feelings.

This is the Holy Spirit at work, the fullness of God as revealed in Jesus' life, ministry, death, and resurrection. The Holy Spirit is God here and now, close by, within our lives. When we receive our hearts, we find God's heart, the life of Jesus alive in us.

Life can be hard, but if we surrender to life's challenges we may run the risk of losing our hearts. If we just give up, then we are neither hot nor cold, and life spews us out of its deepest experience. This is the danger of the great divorce—this is despair.

A LIFELESS CHURCH

The great divorce of the human heart from itself and from Christ is a danger also to the church. The Book of Revelation is a heart book. John's suffering for Christ and the church's persecution by the Roman Empire led John to look into his heart, where he confronted his feelings, fears, and faith. John's experiences produced visions of hope and words of loving admonition to the congregations that he loved.

The church at Laodicea was caught up in the throes of a great divorce. It was separated from its life source, a church in trouble. In seeking to escape pain and suffering, the Laodicean church gave in and accommodated the culture in which it lived. In Christ's warning words that church is described, "I know your deeds, that you are neither cold nor hot. I wish you were either one or the other! So because you are lukewarm—neither hot nor cold—I am about to spit you out of my mouth" (Rev. 3:15–16).

There is no greater judgment than expulsion, because expulsion cuts one off from hope. Expulsion is the worst punishment in school—it means a student is cut off from the power of the whole educational institution and all the vast knowledge of the varied enterprises of the school's history and present connections. The student no longer benefits from relationships with the teachers or fellow students. Expulsion is hopelessness, and expulsion from Christ means all the benefits of grace and God's kingdom are unavailable to the church. It means not being present with Jesus. It means despair.

The Laodicean church was in dire straits. Its sin must have been great—God was ready to expel it from God's presence and purposes. Losing all the benefits of Jesus Christ is a horrific thing to ponder, and we don't usually consider this an option for our parish—just as none of us would ever think it a possibility for our lives.

What could the church at Laodicea have done that was so bad? The people had lost their singular devotion to and passion for Jesus as their Lord. And how had they lost it? The Roman imperial government sought to incorporate and unify its diverse citizens through emperor worship, while also allowing room for other religious expressions. A religion could exist alongside emperor worship if its adherents would confess, "Caesar is Lord," and thereby worship the ruler. The Laodiceans attempted syncretism—their passionate devotion to Jesus was watered down with Caesar worship in order to keep for the church the material blessings of their culture.

The Laodicean Christians were citizens of a wealthy city, and they shared in its wealth. Their hometown was a commercial hub—a textile center specializing in the production of famous black wool garments, with a medical college that offered special medical care. It was hard for the Laodicean Christians to risk losing these material benefits in order to hold onto a singular and passionate devotion to Jesus. Cultural accommodation is an enticing temptation.

Their syncretism went almost unnoticed because the times were so good and they felt so blessed. False security and well-being deceived their hearts. They were moral, they believed in God, and they confessed Jesus. Things were going pretty well for them.

The sad part is that the church was not aware of its own condition. The writer of the letter on behalf of Christ said of them and to them, "You say, 'I am rich; I have acquired wealth and do not need a thing.' But you do not realize that you are wretched, pitiful, poor, blind and naked" (Rev. 3:17).

ACCOMMODATION UNAWARE

It is easier than we think to water down our heart's commitment to Christ. The church is always living in the danger of accommodation—of losing its heart for Jesus. The church can get out of touch with its own heart and the heart of God in the temptation to compromise to both the civil culture and the present culture of religion.

For many years in the United States it has been difficult to distinguish Christian faith from the civil religion of our nation. The church has come to share in the wealth of our affluent American society, which can cause the church to fear the loss of its wealth. It may shy away from an ardent representation of Christ to the world, or from taking a stand contrary to popular opinion expressed in the media or the entertainment industry that so effectively shape public opinion. In our desire to make the church acceptable to more people, we have often compromised its legacy and conformed its life to fit the expectations and desires of the world. Our devotion to Christ and the unique life and witness of the church often give way to our desire to be pleasing to others. Yet it is possible for us to please people and displease God.

The church can lose its power and distinctive call in Christ by accommodating itself to the culture of religion just as easily as to the culture of society. I believe in the holy and ecumenical church, the body of Christ, made up of all baptized, believing, and faith-living Christians. The ecumenical movement that has sought to help all denominational expressions of the church universal work more closely with each other is a grand thing. There is a noble nature in this movement toward unification, but there is also a chance we will lose the heart of good churches which have a powerful witness to offer to the world. Some of the particular and distinctive passion for Christ that lives in these denominations could be sacrificed in accommodating the culture of religion.

In our desire to make the church
acceptable to more people
we have often compromised its legacy
and conformed its life
to fit the expectations and desires of the world.

In the postmodern world in which one community's truth is seen as being as valid as another (whatever religion it happens to be), where there are no transcending truths, values, or moral principles, we find it difficult to claim our own heartfelt truths. Caught up in this new culture of thought and life, we lose confidence in the texts of our own faith. We can easily lose our passion for the Old and New Testaments as a clear and authoritative Word from God to us. We forget our own book trying to honor the books of other communities.

In a time in which we have had trouble affirming the primacy of Christian Scriptures—because we want to be tolerant and accepting of people with other faith traditions and because we are aware of the mystery of God that truly transcends all human understanding—we find ourselves unable to claim with certainty the understanding of God revealed in Jesus Christ. We convince ourselves that to embrace what we obviously believe is true in our faith is an unkind thing that in some way attacks another person's religion. We fear spiritual elitism and arrogance that would devalue another person. We are not convinced that there is some overarching eternal truth for all people and all time. We begin to find it difficult to claim the value of goodness contained in religious texts.

Consider the concept of God revealed by Jesus as "love," that is, selfless love—agape —that is offered humbly but powerfully to forgive and accept every person; whose will is that all persons have eternal life and that love be the first priority of all people—love for God, for each other, and for all creation. There is no higher value than this revelation of the nature of God as declared in Holy Scripture. That progressive revelation grows from ancient radical monotheism until it finally is expressed in the cross and resurrection of Jesus. Surely, this God concept has the power of the Holy Spirit—God present for all ages and people in all circumstances—and is capable of producing a much better life and world than other less tender, less powerful, and less transcending God concepts.

If Christians live by this faith, we will only honor and bless other people. We do not have to deny our own Scriptures to be kind and loving toward people of other faiths. Each of us must claim the highest truth in our religious texts and live that truth toward others with confidence in the integrity of our witness. Much power is returned to the church and to you and me when we live in the courage of this confidence. We must find the freedom to allow our community's text, the Bible, to define us in relationship to others.

In seeking to accommodate the religious culture of this present time, we sometimes lose deep conviction for our own church's faith. We can simmer into lukewarm water and become a church whose heart has stopped beating.

NO SELLING OUT OF AN EMPTY WAGON

We must not preach, teach, or live out of an empty wagon. There was an old familiar saying I heard often when I was growing up: "You can't sell out of an empty wagon." I remember those days as a child when the country store had peddler trucks, and the peddler would roam the graveled roads with groceries, candy, and assorted supplies needed by the farm families. I used to watch for the peddler when I was at my Ma and Pa Fullers' house. Usually Ma would find some way to have a little change on hand with which to buy me a piece of candy—my favorite was a sugar-coated coconut ball. It was such a special treat. Can you imagine how heartbroken I would have been if the peddler pulled up with an empty truck?

Jesus told a parable worthy of remembering. He said that when an evil spirit leaves a person and finds no place to make a home, the evil seeks a void to fill. It returns to the house of the person's life and finds it empty and swept clean—but not occupied. The spirit of evil gathers other, even more wicked powers and they go in and fill the place where no positive affection for high purposes resides. Then the person's life is worse than before (Matt. 12:43–45).

Emptiness cannot provide fullness of hope and life for others. A church can be full of people but empty of heart. A big and bustling congregation can be as much a desperate church as a small one with few people, little programs, and inadequate resources. The principle of death makes no distinction in churches by size or wealth.

Sometimes people come to church looking for life, help, or a message of love and grace—only to find empty lives and empty words. We cannot sell out of an empty wagon. There must be a positive affection in our hearts that expels evil, smallness, selfishness, and self-righteousness that will empower us to make our church and our lives an offering of grace for the salvation of the world. This is the crown and goal of holy passion. If we in the church are not filled with a positive devotion and Jesus-shaped compassion, then evil spirits will come and inhabit our house.

We may find that the church is demonized by competition, emphasis on appearances instead of substance, power conflicts, busyness, selfishness, entering into a survival mode instead of a serving mode, powerlessness, lack of resourcefulness and creativity, poor stewardship, lack of deep spiritual lives, an inward focus, institutionalism and bureaucracy, coldness of heart, over-politicization of decisions, and worship of tradition and ritual.

When not powered by a passion of Christ in the purposes of grace:

- Liberalism becomes a new kind of legalism that cannot get beyond the words of Scripture to the symbolic and metaphorical meaning of the words. Rather than the generosity of spirit and largeness of inclusive love that liberalism claims, it becomes just as exclusive and condemning of those who differ with it as does the far right.

- Instead of bringing new life to the body of Christ, the charismatic experience and the charismatic movement become divisive and exhibit spiritual elitism.

- Traditional Christian expression becomes cold, boring, and lifeless, and exhibits an elitist attitude.

- Born-again Christianity, with a swept-clean house, becomes a shallow appearance of new life and is indifferent to the suffering outsiders of the world.

- Evangelical Christian expression focuses on judgment instead of the redeeming, accepting, and life-changing gospel.

When the spirit of grace and kindly affection for Jesus is not central to the worship of contemporary Christian people, worship resembles a "Pavlovian" conditioned response.

Every church of any denomination or size, rich or poor, can grow divorced from its heart—missing the presence of Christ. Today, we who have had our houses swept clean must invite into this emptiness the passionate power of Christ, the indwelling heart of God, so that God's purposes might enliven the people of God for serving the world.

NEGATING THE NEGATIVITY

These negatives are a life-and-death possibility in all of our churches. They are real and have to be confronted as such. It is easy for us to focus on the negative instead of the life potential of Christ's presence. In my years of serving the church I have sometimes had to fight allowing some small dark cloud of pessimism to shut out the sunlight of all the wonderful things going on in the rest of the church.

We do not need to honor negativity by dwelling on it and giving it too much power. However, we do have to face it and deal with it. Recently I attended a meeting with the men in my church who are active in prayer groups. It was my scheduled teaching time with them, and I planned a session on the "Three Bs of a Compelling Witness," lifting up boldness, boundaries, and balance. At some point in the teaching I said to them that we should not talk so much about Satan—we don't need to honor him that much. We don't need to give evil that much power. In talking about Satan we give evil a power that it does not have over us. Out of all that I shared with these men, this is the one thing that has been referred to the most. It was an unplanned aside that God used to move us from negativity to focusing on the grace and goodness of God that can fill all empty places with the positive affection of noble grace.

Negativity does not produce life. It pushes us down. We have to deal with problems, but our calling is to ministry and new life. I know the dire membership statistics of the mainline churches and those of my denomination. I grieve because members of the church see it as a social club and do not value it more or give more of their time and heart to it. I regularly confront people who believe the church belongs to them and that they are to

If there is anything the church
can claim for new life
it is this . . .
Jesus is the resurrection and the life,
and His help is on the way.

control it and have tantrums if they are not allowed to have their way. I see that some, and sometimes many, give more of their lives and money to sports than to the church to which they have pledged their ultimate loyalty. I am saddened by the continuing racial exclusiveness of congregations and the generally misinformed understanding of the church as something other than the body of Christ in which the heart of God is to be revealed, experienced, and served. I know well the politicization of the local churches and of the national agencies and ruling conferences or judicatories of the old mainline churches. Yet, my love for the church overrules my tendency to dwell on the negatives. Not all congregations of all mainline churches are divorced congregations. The mainline churches read their obituaries regularly in papers and publications and think, *I do not remember my own funeral. I feel like I am still alive and have a lot yet to do.*

Instead of emphasizing these negative realities, I am choosing to focus on Jesus, the center of our faith, as the answer to life for the church. God's positive love for the world that endows the church with its reason for living will guide us in our continued discussion in this book. If there is anything the church can claim for new life it is this unconquered and powerful love. Jesus is the resurrection and the life, and His help is on the way. Lazarus is not hopeless. Divorced from hope, the church sees its restored heart coming—"Jesus-life!"

Chapter Four

SENT FROM THE HEART OF GOD

THE HEART OF GOD INCARNATE—MADE REAL and available in Jesus—is the divine presentation of unmerited and unconditional love. This is the heart that enlivens the body of Christ. The character and power of this grace in the life of the church is meant to give witness to God's creative availability and to God's continuing love and faithfulness. It is this grace, the revealed heart of God, which births, sustains, and enables the life and ministry of the church. It is the power source of the Lazarus church raised to new life.

Jesus is grace made real, the heart of God given to us to bring God's creative power into our lives. It is this power of redemption that the church holds in its heart. Whether it is a small or a large congregation, the true power of new life is the experience and manifestation of Christ-love. This is the power of Jesus to birth people into a new life of abundance and hope. Paul said, "Therefore, if anyone is in Christ, he is a new creation; the old has gone, the new has come!" (2 Cor. 5:17). If this potential becomes the focus and purpose of a congregation, then it is a Lazarus church raised up to lift up others. Love becomes incarnate when people who suffer experience the divine heart in a congregation's deeds and words.

Richard was a man who lived in the community of my first pastorate. He was a man's man—an outdoorsman and not so much impressed with the church or his need of what it offered. His wife, however, was our organist and his sons attended our church. Richard sometimes joked about the hypocrites at the church; he and I enjoyed our bantering and had a relationship that was friendly and cordial.

Richard began having severe headaches. He was hospitalized for tests, and a brain tumor was discovered. During his operation, the surgeon told Richard's family that he could not remove the entire tumor for fear of doing more damage to Richard. In the ensuing weeks and months of Richard's successful recovery from his cancer, the congregation sent cards, prepared food, visited, and truly befriended Richard and his family with the friendship of Christ. Through the love of the people, Jesus came close to Richard and the gospel became real. One Sunday during the invitational hymn, Richard, walking with a cane, came forward and committed himself to Jesus and to the church. He wanted to be baptized in the creek behind his house. He invited all of his family and friends, which was most of that rural community. With his one good arm, Richard built a bridge across a ravine so folks could cross over to the creek and participate in his baptism. I have never seen or known a more changed life.

Some years later, Richard's family called me to the hospital. As Richard was drawing near to death, I asked him a question I had never asked anyone in such a state before. "If you could ask God for anything and God would grant it right now, what would you ask for?" Richard thought a minute and said, "I guess I already have it. I am a child of God."

This is the power of grace made real in Jesus— the incarnate heart of God given for Lazarus ministries. Churches that participate in Jesus' ministry of birthing new Christians become enlivened themselves and their pastors are transformed. All within this type of witness are encouraged and their faith is made strong to serve the Lord. This grace is at the heart of a Lazarus church to create life.

The heart power of the church is sustained by its witness to the continuing faithfulness of God expressed in the life, death, and resurrection of

Jesus. The heart of God in the life of a congregation declares that the mercy of the Lord is from everlasting to everlasting. Jesus proclaims in word and deed, in life and in eternity that God is like a loving father to God's children. This heart message of the church calls the Lazarus congregation to never give up on itself, its people, or any desperate soul in a world teeming with violence, aggression, hate, racism, greed, injustice, and sin of every strain. God does not give up. God can come in Jesus to the tomb of utter agony and grief and declare in death's bold face that there is still One who loves and can restore life. This is the message of continuing hope and possibilities in the heart power of the church's ministry and community of grace.

FOCUS

This past Christmas I gave my wife a nice camera. It is somewhat complex, but it's supposed to take great photographs. It has an automatic focus that can also be set manually, along with other features that allow her to take a variety of pictures. When my wife first used the camera she did pretty well, but she could have done better. She was having some trouble with the focus, which she needed to use in order to be more creative with her photography. She eagerly enrolled in a photography class that came as a bonus with the purchase of the camera. During the class she learned how to set the camera to catch water in a fountain as it was falling through the air as if it stood still—that was an amazingly beautiful picture. Such beauty could not come with automatic focus. It could come only with a focus that was determined and intentional.

So it is with Christ and us, with the church and its vital life. So much of the power of the Christian and of the church does not come with automatic focus—we have to choose the right focus to find the grace to be God's people and Christ's church.

True Lazarus churches focus on Jesus' love and confess the faith that Jesus is the Son of God, the Savior of the world, and the Lord of all.

In the story of the raising of dead Lazarus to life, the possibility arose when Mary and Martha changed their focus from the power of death to the power of Christ to bring life. They saw Jesus' love for Lazarus in His coming to Bethany during their time of grief and in Jesus' tears beside the tomb. They claimed the truth of Christ and Martha expressed it by her confession, "Yes, Lord, I believe that you are the Messiah, the Son of God, the one coming into the world" (John 11:27). Focused on the love of Jesus and the truth of Christ, Mary and Martha saw Jesus' power when he said in a loud voice, "Lazarus, come out!" (John 11:43). That day Martha and Mary saw the glory of the Lord; that is, they experienced the presence of the highest God who raises the dead to life.

True Lazarus churches focus on Jesus' love and confess the faith that Jesus is the Son of God, the Savior of the world, and the Lord of all. They experience the power of God in Christ and the glory of God, and they become vitally alive because their focus is true. It is not something that just happens because the church is the church or because we are Christians—we have to train our focus by seeking Christ. We must find ourselves in discipline and devotion to Christ, from whom vital piety and strong life flows and in whom all things come into beautiful focus. The great message God gives to the church is not a doctrine or a philosophy or some kind of ideal; it is Jesus—God's heart revealed.

THE CENTER THAT HOLDS

Our faith is Christ-centered. Jesus is the hub of our hope and of our ability to run effectively in His service. If Christ is not centermost in the life of the church, we begin to wobble about and wander into dangerous ditches or side paths.

When I was a boy growing up in the country there was not much to do but work on the farm, visit at the country store, go to school, attend church, play ball, and ride bicycles. The boys of Lascassas, Tennessee, and another nearby village, Cainesville, built dirt tracks in each community, and we would alternate Sunday afternoons between the two communities for races. That meant preparing our bicycles. We did not have the fancy bicycles of today—ours were often put together with parts from many old bikes. Sometimes my wheels would wobble and not run true, so I would have to turn my bike upside down under a shade tree and tighten every spoke to the hub of the wheel. If I got each spoke equally tight, the wheels would run smooth and straight, and I would have a chance to ride a good race.

Today, in life's race and in the church's witness, we are encouraged to tighten our spokes. Ever so often we need to ratchet the outer part of the wheels of the church and of our lives more tightly to the center. The author of Hebrews admonishes us, "Let us fix our eyes on Jesus, the author and perfecter of our faith, who for the joy set before him endured the cross . . ." (Heb. 12:2). Yes, we look to Jesus as the true heart of our lives. The church—the realm and sphere of the congregation's life and influence— seeks and needs a passion power for God that is centered on Jesus and unleashed by the Holy Spirit.

BEGIN WITH THE HEART OF GOD

Where then does the parish, and indeed where do you and I begin to help the church gain and keep a passionate power for life, for the world, for God, and for God's kingdom? We begin with the hope of all the ages—the heart of God made incarnate in Jesus Christ. We begin with the grace of God made real—the incarnate Word of God made flesh in the life of Jesus.

The idea of the incarnation not only speaks of the *logos*, mind or reason of God, it also has to do with revealing the heart of God—God's innermost presence. The words of John the evangelist about the "Word becoming flesh" include grace and truth. The Word made flesh is described as being "full of grace and truth" (John 1:14).

I suppose none of us is ever satisfied with knowing the truth about another person to whom our heart reaches out—we hunger to learn their thoughts and feelings toward us. How grand it is when we reach out in affection and passion to another, and we are met not with cold reason or ideas, but with an open heart until we know and experience the person's feelings for us. The sharing of these feelings for us can so fire our hearts that we become accessible, vulnerable, and transparent to our beloved.

Someone always has to take the first risk when two hearts open to one another. This is a fearful thing to do. Yet God did that very thing—God acted first. God put God's love and life in Jesus, and declared God to us. Jesus in His humanity held and revealed the fullness of God. His humanity overflowed with the divine love that is powerful to win our hearts, to hold us, and to free us.

When Jesus died on the cross, the veil of the temple was torn in two—providing a passage into the innermost holy place with God. We have, because of this life and death of Jesus, come to know we can stand in the "holy of holies"—the very presence of God.

To stand in such a place with our lives is to stand near the heart of God. "There is a place of quiet rest, near to the heart of God; a place where sin cannot molest, near to the heart of God. There is a place of full release, near to the heart of God." The power of our Christian lives and of the parish is expressed in the chorus to this wonderful old hymn. "O Jesus blest Redeemer, sent from the heart of God, hold us who wait before thee near to the heart of God."[8]

In Jesus' death the veil that hides God's feelings for us is pulled back and God is made transparent and accessible. Because of God's love for us born from eternity, God is now exposed on that hillside in Jesus' suffering. From there God flings infinite and perfect love to us in absolute abandonment. The appeal of this cross of grace is God's plea that such divine love might lodge itself in our hearts and save us.

This passion of God in Christ is God's gift to us. It becomes the motive power for our living as Christians, and it is the strange and grand power of the church. This is God's gift for the world's salvation.

That which is revealed in Jesus is nothing new—there was no moment when God's love for us changed. The cross of Jesus raised on Calvary and the dying form upon it is the lifting of the veil around God's heart. That cross in history is the cross of suffering love that has been in the heart of God for humankind since the foundations of the earth. God has always loved us with suffering love—the love that is like a parent's love.

We have, because of this life and death of Jesus,
come to know we can stand in the
"holy of holies"—the very presence of God.

Years ago I was serving a church in a suburban community. It was Christmas morning, and I went out and got the paper before anyone else got up. As I drank my cup of coffee, my heart was saddened when I read the headline story of a young man shot down while committing an armed robbery at a nearby convenience store. I knew the man and his family; his parents were members of the church I served. He was in the intensive care unit of a local hospital, hanging onto life by a thread. As I drove to the hospital I thought of the embarrassment of the family. How would they greet me? When I went into the waiting room, they rushed to me and held onto me. I represented their church—and in some way Jesus. More than who I am walked into that room with me that day; the church and the Savior accompanied me. The boy's father and I went up to the intensive care unit. The room was relatively dark. As he reached behind the curtain to hold his son's hand, the father began to weep. He took out his handkerchief and wiped his eyes—the father saw his son's danger and pain and suddenly the betrayal didn't matter—he still loved his son. We prayed, and as I was leaving I looked back around the curtain and was deeply moved by a scene of unending love: the father was wiping the face of his son with his tear-stained handkerchief. I thought to myself, *That is how God loves us. God never gives up on us.*

God's love on the cross is the divine love of the parent who longs for her or his wayward and hurting child to know the power and joy of life. When our children are sinful, lost from the goodness of life, burdened, confused, trouble to others and to themselves, we do not curse them or judge them. Our hearts bleed for them. A searing cross is raised in our hearts. So it is in the heart of God for us that was made reality in Christ. The "Word made flesh" in Jesus makes the heart of God real to us.

God seeks to continue the incarnation of this eternal heart of grace and to make it real for the world in the life of the church. God works to birth such a heart within God's people—within your heart and mine. The Holy Spirit seeks to make this love visible, touchable, tangible, and active in every level of the church's life.

This is the source of the passion power of the parish. This is the energy that compels congregations and the institutions of the churches to live and serve with warmth, with deep emotion, with ardent love, and with boundless enthusiasm for the purposes of Christ. This is the heart power that can raise a Lazarus church and fling a message of light into the world's darkness. Jesus is sent to us to birth and sustain the church from the heart of God.

LOOKING FOR A HOME

Jesus is always looking for a home in this world. When He was born in a cave in Bethlehem, God became available and vulnerable. The circumstances of the time put Jesus' family in a situation to be away from home, and they were not invited into any one else's home.

Mary and Joseph had come from Nazareth to Bethlehem in obedience to the decree of the Roman government. They went to Bethlehem so that the one upon whose shoulders the "government of the kingdom of God would rest" might enter the realm of His reign of grace.

Although this mystery cast its holiness around their lives, they could not fully know the incredible import of their journey, which may have seemed to them merely a bothersome obedience to the laws of human government.

Mary and Joseph perhaps had little suspicion of the glory of the One given to them—although they had had dreams and had heard angels' voices. Such things sink back into the abyss of human subconsciousness when our duty and doings take strong hold of us, when fear and pain crouch at our door. But God moves within the strange decrees, policies, and powers of earth, and in our just doing what we have to do. God works even there to bring forth the birth of salvation.

When Jesus was born, His family could not go home. Within two years they were forced to flee to Egypt to guard and preserve God's invasion of earth—lest the governments of the earth cast God out of the world too soon. God's delivering and saving power would come as it had come once before, "out of Egypt" in the form of a homeless and wandering family in whom all the families of the world could find their hope of being God's people.

When Jesus was fulfilling His ministry He did not have a home. He was an itinerant preacher moving about to be with the people who needed God's love most. In some unfathomable manner this was God looking for a home with God's people, that they might have the benefits of the heart of God. This heart's search never will be over until all people welcome God into their deepest, most personal, and most intimate lives.

Jesus said back then and still says, "Foxes have their holes and birds of the air have nests, but the Son of Man has no place to lay his head" (Matt. 8:20). Jesus is still looking for a home in the world—in your personal world and mine. The home Jesus seeks is our hearts. Jesus seeks to be born in us—to indwell our hearts with the heart of God—to bring God's love forth in human life.

Jesus seeks to live His life again in us that He might continue to be God's offering to the world. Jesus seeks this place in our hearts that His life might be formed in us and lived through us—made touchable, approachable, vulnerable, and available in the world for the world! There is nothing more personal than that which lives in our hearts. Jesus said, "For where your treasure is, there your heart will be also" (Matt. 6:21).

Jesus seeks a house not made with hands. He seeks a house created by God for Him to live and have His being in—to reveal God's own life. The house of our lives and our hearts is Jesus' true home. This Jesus-shaped room cannot welcome other guests. It is His place in this world just as the holes are the place for the foxes and just as the nests are the place for the birds. If Jesus is not at home with us, then we are not at home in this life and something is always missing. We are not fully alive, and the world misses the gift we are meant to give.

UP CLOSE AND PERSONAL WITH JESUS

We are asked to get up close and personal with Jesus, that He might have His life in us for the world. Oh how grand it would be for you and me, for the church and for the world, if we could say with the same conviction and sincerity what the apostle Paul said about himself, "I no longer live, but Christ lives in me. The life I live in the body, I live by faith in the Son of God, who loved me and gave himself for me" (Gal. 2:20).

Being up close and personal with Jesus means having Him at home in our hearts and allowing His life to be lived in us. In this home Jesus has a place from which to enter the world for His ongoing salvation purposes. Being up close and personal with Jesus means He must be our focus. We must gaze upon Him until we see Him clearly and, upon seeing Him, welcome Him home.

In order for the church to experience and become the passion of Jesus, we who make up the church must believe in and experience Jesus as One who is real in our hearts. We must embrace Jesus' life, death, resurrection, and ascension as the saving events of God. These acts of God are the nail on which the hopes of the world hang. Jesus is not an idea or a doctrine, although Christology—the theology of Jesus—is essential to who we are and must be clearly defined and fully known. But Jesus is more. Jesus is the personal and superpersonal power of God indwelling human life. Jesus, by the graceful reality of the Holy Spirit, is able to be here and now. This means salvation is not long ago and far away, but a present power.

---

*Being up close and personal with Jesus
means He must be our focus.
We must gaze upon Him until we
see Him clearly and, upon seeing Him,
welcome Him home.*

Christ is both immanent and transcendent, the person of God living intimately with us, witnessing to the fullness of God. When we experience the presence of God, the moment transcends all time, space, history, and our current experience. This One who can spiritually invade and take up residence in our consciousness is the Jesus of history—not a storybook character but One who really lived in Palestine with real people who looked Him in the eyes. This is the One who stood in our human condition and sanctified it by overcoming its weaknesses, its sins, and its death. We can visit the sites of His life and walk among the trees He prayed under and sit on the rocks on which He sat. Jesus is real.

Although we do not know a lot of details about Jesus, we do perceive Him through the eyes of others who have made up the church from the first day of His life and throughout His ministry. We have from His mother and from His disciples stories that were passed down verbally and by gospel writers. We are indebted to the more than five hundred who witnessed His postresurrection appearances—to these same people who knew of His death and were now confronted by His living presence.

Across all the ages we are given this one solitary hope of every person of every age, as He has lived across the centuries within human hearts who spoke His life to us in words and deeds of mercy and truth. No church can be a true Lazarus church until its members are captivated by the truth that God's heart message is revealed in a person.

This person is the Christ of God, the Lord of history, and the Savior of the world. He is an important person to get to know. You will be impressed, and you'll want others to know you have met Him. One day you and I will see that every knee will bow and every tongue confess that Jesus Christ is Lord (Phil. 2:10–11). We will never meet anyone more important. He is the best known and greatest celebrity of the ages, and He can and will go home with you. Jesus will take you home with Him when your day on earth is done. This One can be nearer to you than your breath, closer to you than your skin. He can live your life with you.

Jesus is life and love and hope. Jesus can make our life a gift to the world—a treasure trove of abundant grace that opens to others as they look to us for help and love and friendship. This great reality of the person of God given to the world who takes up His life within us gives us the power of a personal witness. The indwelling Christ is the inspiration of the corporate life of the church empowering its proclamation of hope to the world. This One who came to earth bearing the heart of God gives the resurrection and life-infusing power needed to make Lazarus churches live gloriously with servant love and sacrificial grace.

RESTORED HEART

If our hearts are alienated from the great center of all life—the heart of God, in whom we only find peace—then where do we turn for help? If we have lost sight of our own hearts in the false fables of earthly promises, how can our hearts be restored? If our churches are lifeless bodies without passion, how can they be set free from the grave clothes of unfeeling?

We turn to the Christ who knocks at the door. The fact that Christ stands at the door and knocks is judgment and grace—fear and salvation. Jesus does not appear to be someone we would want to let in— He brings with Him the lantern of truth that reveals things as they really are, but He also brings the salve of grace that heals and helps. We must first face His truth: no cure for the soul of the church or for you or me can come without the revealing diagnosis of where we are broken and the recognition of our sinfulness and need of redemption. The door of truth has to be opened for healing and transformation to come into our hearts.

In Revelation 3:14–22, Jesus is presented as the One with authority and power to confront the church with its diseased heart—its neediness before God. He is the One who is the faithful witness—full of God's truth and life, grace and love. He is the Amen—the one true and dependable Word of God for us. Jesus has a right to the house because of the authority of His person.

Jesus has another kind of authority. It is the authority of One who loves those in the house, who has the right to enter our lives because He cares enough for us to gain entrance. His love for us has been proven.

Jesus comes worthily to the door, yet He approaches us both sternly and tenderly. His truth rebukes us, admonishes us, and tells us to change our lives and to reform the life of the church. He cares for us in our present condition but He does not wish for us to remain as we are. He comes with a light in His hand to expose our sick and malnourished lives; and with spiritual bread to nourish us back to wholeness. Jesus will eat and drink with us until we are strong and until the church has its heart again, until the passion for the Savior returns to our hearts to sustain us.

No one can treat our hearts without our consent. Consenting to let Jesus in cures the heart of the church. Surrendering once again to Jesus returns the fire of passion to the furnace of faith—the heart restored to love for Christ. We have in many of our worship services been invited to accept Jesus, receive Jesus, or to choose Jesus. Sometimes we know what all this means—and sometimes not. Although these are valid invitations, if we are to become truly Christian and if the church is to be His, we must fully yield to Jesus and let Him have His way with the church and with us.

When we yield to Jesus He restores us and unites us with God's love. In this restoration we find the motive power of a heartfelt faith that awakens the church to new vitality. When Jesus has His way with the church, the will of God becomes the church's central focus and new devotion sustains its enthusiasm for life, for the needy world, and for the ministry of Christ's outreaching love. The church is thereby compromised no more and, instead of being conformed to the world, the church begins to transform the world.

Chapter Five

CHURCH
UNBOUND

THE LAZARUS CHURCH RELEASED FROM THE CAVE and unbound is a world-transforming force. It is people freed to serve the world with a graceful and powerful presence that takes hold of weak lives to stand them up in the presence of Jesus. They meet with the One who alone has the power to peer into the caves of their lives—where darkness prevails—to call them out into the light of God's possibilities which are mysteriously unlimited.

Some churches are caught up in a dull and listless kind of worship. They hold onto each other as if they are afraid to take the next step lest they walk off into some dark rift in their landscape. They seem to constantly bump their heads on some hidden roof that will not allow them to experience the grand vision of God. However, Jesus has a desire and a power to deliver such churches into the light of a world where everything good and grace-filled is possible.

I once took a youth group into the caves at the foot of Ben Lomand Mountain outside McMinnville, Tennessee. We left the bright world of light for the day, and in that cavern there was absolute darkness. We could not see our hands in front of our faces when we touched our own noses. The darkness was thick and smothering, and although we moved close to one another, we were afraid. A guide with a flashlight led us to a room where there were some dangling electric bulbs. There was unnatural light, but it wasn't sufficient. The light reflected off us and the rocks around us to form dark and foreboding shadows against the walls of the cave. Although we stayed in that cave all day, we never completely adjusted to the darkness.

As their pastor, I felt responsible for the group. I wished I had some light that was adequate, but in hindsight I know that they would never have appreciated the light without first experiencing the darkness. There was light outside waiting for us to emerge from the cave, but we were not in it. I looked forward to the moment when I would lead them out of the cave into that light. I felt almost starved for light—God's natural sunlight.

By mid-afternoon my group was led out of the cave. I exited first so I could welcome the group into the sunshine. At first the light was blinding, and we could hardly look up; but when our eyes adjusted we felt an overpowering astonishment at the beauty we had forgotten. There were no frightening shadows—the sky was blue and the clouds were white and fluffy. The green grass was amazingly alive, and the mountains and even the highway at the end of the driveway were a wonder to behold. We were captivated by the beauty of the world when the light of God's Spirit cast out the darkness and revealed it to us.

Churches that dwell in the darkness lit only by human intellect and the creation of human thought and speculation, guided by political posturing, bureaucracy, and tradition know a paralysis of spirit that is debilitating to the mission purposes of Christ. Too many churches live in the "shadow lands" of faith and mission.

The forces of evil would love to keep the church in its cave—confused and unable to experience or serve the beauty of the light of God. What a terrible thing if the church of the Lord were to live in the cave, wrapped in the trimmings of religion, without the light of truth and grace to inspire it to act courageously.

But there is light. God, who promises new creation—new life—said, "Let there be light," and there was light (Gen. 1:3). After the death of Saul and the victory of David, the people who had been in conflict went to their villages and homes. It was said at that time, "After that, God answered prayer in behalf of the land" (2 Sam. 21:14). Soon thereafter David and the people had a great battle with the Philistines. After victory in battle David sang a song of praise and faith to the Lord in which he exulted, "You are my lamp, O Lord; the Lord turns my darkness into light" (2 Sam. 22:29). Jesus said, "I am the light of the world. Whoever follows me will never walk in darkness, but will have the light of life" (John 8:12).

Jesus, like God in creation, inaugurates the new Kingdom Age and calls us into His light by the authority of His Word. He compels the church to step from its frightful cavernous darkness into His brilliant light. There he reveals the wrappings of death that hold us and commands these grave clothes be removed so that we might do His will and live His life of grace and eternity. Jesus' Word is filled with all the meaning of the ancient covenant, grounded in the origins of the faith of Israel and God's eternal and unchanging purposes. Jesus' Word is formed by His people—their truths, mistakes, and lessons learned—and their higher calling in the midst of their failures.

When Lazarus is raised to life he does not return to a town of strangers. He is not sent to Nazareth or Capernaum or Jericho or even to Jerusalem. Lazarus is restored to life in Bethany where all had known he was surely dead—it was here that his being raised from death would have its greatest impact. He comes into the light and experiences new life as an outgrowth of his old life. He gathers with his sisters at the family table according to his ancestor's traditions. He comes from a cave of darkness at the word of a Messiah who came to fulfill the ancient word or traditions that held onto the light of truth.

The unbinding of the Lazaruses of the church world would be a returning to the ancient light that does not fade away. Lazarus in his new life found grace in the old places and power from the rocks from which he was hewn. When the stone released him it was within the light of One who proclaimed an ancient hope.

It is Jesus, the Ancient of Days, who has seen and conquered the darkness, who has the power to call the church into the light so it can enter gloriously into the work of the kingdom of God. This Lord returns the Lazarus church to freedom in God's eternal purposes—God's will. The Lazarus church returned to its true life finds liberty to move into and out of its source, God, and all the original sources of faith and knowledge into ever-greater expressions of life and light. Jesus calls the church out of the cave of its forgetfulness and sets it free for great service and mission.

Like the youth group who entered with me into the darkness of the cave, the Lazarus church called into the light is invited into a world once known which it left behind to enter the darkness. This turning loose into the light is a kind of homecoming that empowers the Lazarus churches raised up and unbound for the adventure ahead.

---

*Jesus calls the church
out of the cave of its forgetfulness
and sets it free for great service and mission.*

One of the things Lazarus gained according to John's gospel was great joy. Lazarus was raised not as a stranger with some kind of emotional and spiritual amnesia, but as a more brilliant experience of himself. His celebration with family and friends and with Jesus at the table in his home was a return that would lead Lazarus into the unfolding glory of the Lord in this world.

This is the call of the Lord to the Lazarus churches of our world—to light and to home and then into the world with the ancient truth, power, and promises of God empowering them to serve God gladly and effectively. Out of the cave and unbound, Lazarus churches are a powerhouse of movement, activity, grace, and life.

OUR ROCK: OUR PRESENT PARISH

There seems always to be a returning to something in renewal and rebirth. Neither people nor churches are conceived or born in a vacuum where God is not— God was in the world before us and before our congregations. God did much in the lives of others before we were thought of, and they have held in their strange and sometimes suffering lives something of God's life that has reached out to take hold of us. Even when the people and churches of our origins were troubled and confused, perhaps holding within something sinful and hurtful, God was present in them for us. This is true of our families, our communities, and our churches and their texts of faith.

When we leave the cave and are released from the grave bindings and restored to right relatedness to God and life—to righteousness—God gives us a new heart. The changed heart is made soft and pliable by God's own grace, and we experience a readiness to see and claim the gifts of grace we had once overlooked.

The prophet Isaiah gave this call from God to God's people, "Listen to me, you who pursue righteousness and who seek the Lord: Look to the rock from which you were cut and to the quarry from which you were hewn; look to Abraham, your father, and to Sarah, who gave you birth" (Isa. 51:1–2).

When God gives the church and its people a new heart, God's Spirit moves us into our lives, not out of them. The new flows out of the old. Paul gives us the promise that ". . . if anyone is in Christ, he is a new creation; the old has gone, the new has come!" (2 Cor. 5:17). Paul is talking about the darkness passing away and the old sin done away with,

the old way of thinking and desiring and doing—
freedom from the grave clothes. We return to our life
and find in it the things of God we had not claimed
and we discover our true lives. This is true of the
individual and it is true of the Lazarus church.

We are promised a new heart for ourselves and
for the people of God with whom we live and serve.
Through Ezekiel, God says to all the Lazarus churches
and their members:

> For I will take you out of the nations; I will gather you
> from all the countries and bring you back into your own
> land. I will sprinkle clean water on you, and you will be
> clean; I will cleanse you from all your impurities and
> from all your idols. I will give you a new heart and put
> a new spirit in you; I will remove from you your heart of
> stone and give you a heart of flesh. And I will put my
> Spirit in you and move you to follow my decrees and be
> careful to keep my laws (Ezek. 36:24–27).

This new heart is a humble heart that can listen and
be taught. It is a seeing heart that has a different
perspective on the experiences, circumstances, and
people of one's life. It is amazing to me that when
they are awakened and step into the light, people
who have occupied pews for years speak of hearing
about God's grace as if they had never heard about it
before. I know better, for I have preached it to them
strongly and often, and their church has held grace

as the central message of its life. Now returned to the rocks from which they were cut, they see what shaped them as they could not see it before. So it goes in Lazarus churches and with Lazarus people— what they had previously missed or despised is now one of the greatest blessings they have ever received.

The parish you and I live our lives of faith with now—all of its history and practices—is a gift of God's heart to us. It is our Bethany. We must receive this gift of our church with thanksgiving so that it can be more for us than we ever imagined it could be. The congregation and the denomination we relate to has a membership made up of people like you and me. That is why it is so often in such a mess. That is also why it is such a grand place to be when God's magnificent grace breaks in on us and we get a glimpse of the church's place in God's plans for us.

Right here in this local parish is where God's heart seeks to meet the world. The local parish, however imperfect it is, is the most important place in the church. It is here that everything in the church either is birthed, acted on, or sustained by its gifts and resources. The local congregation is the vital link in the great world churches and of denominations. If this link is gone, there is no chain.

It is sad that in recent years the "big picture items" of the general church have often minimized the local parish. The issues that divide and confuse the denominations and confound the world as it seeks to understand us shove the good-heartedness of the local parish into the shadows. The local church is often the forgotten parish, but this is changing. The people are refusing to be ignored or pushed aside any longer.

The local church knows how to love and incorporate the people whose lives fail to reflect and even contradict the values of the gospel of Jesus—even when the parish knows that a life is being lived that is not in keeping with the ideals of Christian teaching. Down here the people know we are all saved by grace. In this lowly place, members are willing to worship and serve with all kinds of folks, but draw the line at leadership. The local church seeks and expects the highest qualities in leadership. This sets the tone for the rest of the church as it should, and avoids the spectre of "cheap grace."

Although we don't want to embrace what is unacceptable to Christian teaching, we do not have to agree with or affirm someone's lifestyle or compromise any high value in order to include people in our hearts. Down here we can just give our hearts to one another. Down here we know how sinful we all are and how we are dependent upon the heart of God for our hope. Maybe the heart of God is alive in the local church first and foremost.

Yet down here we need the resolutions, theology, and social principles of the church connected and bound in the world to keep us from getting lost in our hearts to the point that we love others without giving the guidance that can lead them to fullness of life. These guiding truths, however, must never rob us in the parish of the suffering heart of God who bears with us so that we might bear with others. We are never called to be ugly or mean toward God's children. We are called to hold true to God with gentleness, kindness, and mercy. We who know how life is for us and could be for us without Jesus must patiently and gracefully reach out to others—with truth, yes, but not without grace. Such balance of the passionate heart and the informed conscience best encounters the world through the local church.

Too often the church leadership has looked upon the local laity and local clergy as unsophisticated—not too smart and certainly out of touch with true wisdom and knowledge. The passionate heart of the local parish is often left without a voice or sense of significance in the larger realm of the church. On the other hand, we of the local parish can get pretty self-righteous toward the general church. We often do not give the leadership of the church the due consideration that they are at least as Christian as the rest of us. We see these leaders as politically motivated social philosophers rather than servants searching for the heart of Jesus. Too often we fail to relate to one another—it seems to always be the agenda or the issue that brings us together.

None of this is intentional. It just sort of happens when we stop listening to each other's hearts and get so caught up in who is right and who is wrong or who is going to control the future. Maybe God is the One who stands for the future, and our lot would best be cast with the heart of God—Jesus Christ—who pulls back the veil to reveal the suffering love of God. It may be that here we can truly discover each other.

There will be no raising or releasing
of the Lazarus church
if on the front line the local church
remains in the cave,
wrapped in the cloths of death.

If we could receive our local parish and our denomination as a gift from God, we would gain so much. Here again we need not be put off by the specifics—we can listen to the broad and general offerings of God in the uniqueness that is in our parish. We can ask questions of the history of the parish and listen for the heart truths that have shaped it. What does it really care about? How did it come to be the way it is? What is it God seems to be doing in bringing this congregation to be as it now is, and what is God seeking to have our parish become and do? The parish's truth can be God's call and blessing on our lives. There will be no raising or releasing of the Lazarus church if on the front line the local church remains in the cave, wrapped in the cloths of death.

I believe that in the core of its being, the church is a blessing God wants to give to the world. I believe we need to listen to the church to which we belong—we need to help it claim and live by its heart. The changed heart is a listening heart. When we together hear from the heart of grace, excitement and enthusiasm for God and God's world enliven our hearts.

When Lazarus was raised and returned he must have seen old things in new ways. He must have appreciated God's gifts in his life more completely and he must have pondered what it meant to proclaim and serve God's possibilities revealed to him in Jesus his friend—and now Lord. God's call to the Lazarus church and its members is to see old things in new ways.

PROPAGATE THE POTENTIALITIES

The basic potential of the church is theological. More than a church needs gimmicks, it needs passionate theology—a divine truth to share with the world. We can devise wonderful liturgies with moving experiences and powerful participation where everyone connects with everyone else and still not bring people to a life-transforming experience of God's grace. We can have the grandest high church service and feel aesthetically satisfied and uplifted without finding anything of God's life-giving power in our hearts.

Without the urgently expressed theological proclamation of Jesus Christ, God's love power present in Holy Spirit nearness, we merely entertain and stroke people in the places they hurt without moving them deep into the life of their souls or outward in Jesus' redeeming love for others.

Christian theology that declares a God of grace—not of war or condemnation—is essential. It is the present power that enables us to claim, reproduce, and make known the potentialities God is declaring in this moment and in this place for the church today—not in some last day long past or long coming, but in the here and now. These potentialities do truly reside in the Lazarus church! Although often hidden, they reside in the traditions, words, and longings of the church. We make them into life-less idols, seal them in a cave, and protect them with a stone. We must let them out in the power of what and whom they represent. Today, there resides in the rock of the church from which we are hewn the power to serve the present age.

Why the church often cannot see the great time in which we now serve is confusing to me. I think maybe it's because we don't focus on the glorious personal implications of our theology or ask, "What is God saying to us today? Where is God at work in our church and in our community—in people's

lives? How can we join God in what God is doing?"
Prayerfully pursued, these questions can open our
eyes and move us out of the Lazarus tombs that hold
the "seeking-to-live" congregations.

People all around our churches are openly
exhibiting a spiritual hunger in ways I have not seen
before in my lifetime. Spirituality is a hot topic, and
people where I live and serve are strangely receptive
to an experience of a loving God. Today is one of the
best times the church has ever had to move into the
world and gather the harvest.

Suffering, troubled people who know they are
needy are all around our churches. Homeless people
and poor people looking not only for help but also
for value in life provide a great opportunity. Families
torn apart cry out, knowing there must be help some-
place. These people are valued human beings. If we
would reach out to them with unconditional love,
they would beat a path into the church next week.

The fields are white, and the potential is great. We
have amazing technology available. We have people
in our congregations who, if invited, will do ministry
that clergy and leaders are not as well equipped to do.
These people will give and can empower more
ministries if properly challenged and if we who are
leaders catch and cast the vision of Christ with them.

I am in my twelfth year at the church I now
serve. It has grown steadily during my tenure. It is a
church with a long history and was for many years

a Sunday morning program church. It is now a seven-day-a-week ministry congregation. It has a long tradition of being clergy-centered in expectation of ministry. After studying other churches inside and outside our denomination, we introduced and launched a program called "The Master's Plan—Every Member in Ministry." I taught a Wednesday evening study called "The Master's Plan For Me" in which we explored our personal giftedness and the gifts of the Holy Spirit. We had a churchwide commitment Sunday in which around four hundred people signed up to serve in over 250 ministries. When we launched our training for these people we had a lunch in the gym. More people showed up than had signed up to be there. We didn't have enough chairs and tables, and we ran out of food. It was exciting! Compare what can be done with these hundreds to what a staff of nine can do. This is our first step toward a goal of having a majority of the members doing ministry, not attending meetings. Old mainline churches with long histories and traditions can be Lazarus churches and free the lay members to be raised up in ministry. A congregation does not have to be large in numbers to have such a freeing experience.

I have served small, middle-sized, and large membership churches. I have served a congregation that had a total of ten members, and I have served charges with as many as five congregations as part of the circuit. I grew up in a very small congregation, and I can promise you that small churches have some members who read the same books, watch the same television programs, and go to the same movies as people in the large churches. They are high school and college graduates (having attended the same universities as those in large churches), and will send their children off to colleges and universities. Even where this is not the case, they are well-informed and have been students of life and of the communities of which they are part. They read the same Bible and believe in the same Jesus Christ. Their hearts are as potentially alive in the Spirit of Christ as any person in any great cathedral church or any powerful contemporary church. With pastoral leadership that is secure and willing to get in touch with other leaders and books and with a willingness to grow and learn, the lay members of any church can hear God's call and find their own ministry in the church. There may only be a handful of them, but what a mighty force they could be in a small community!

Remember, Jesus ministered to the multitudes but spent His time shaping the lives of twelve for a ministry that He envisioned to be to all nations. The intimate ministry of grace one-on-one and in small groups is so powerful that large congregations seek ways to divide the people into intimate classes and prayer and ministry groups. Perhaps this is one of Wesley's legacies for today. A Lazarus church with a Lazarus pastor is a mighty thing large or small. It is a lay-involved and led ministry. The people are the power when they discover a passion for Jesus Christ and are enlivened with their own experience of God awakening their hearts. With their own lives renewed, they sound the trumpet of hope to others.

> *The people are the power*
> *when they discover a passion for Jesus Christ*
> *and are enlivened with their own experience*
> *of God awakening their hearts.*

Although most mainline congregations face a changing economy and an aging population, our churches have millions and millions of dollars available to us if we can help people find an encounter with God and discover the grace of Jesus Christ that is seeking them. People find a freedom to give when they experience the compassion of Jesus, the burning zeal of godly love for others, and worship services that lead them on the journey from their heads into their hearts. Churches have to spend money in ministry in order for people to give money. If a church is not making an offering of its life in mission and ministry, then people are not interested in giving. Like a business has to spend money to make money, a church has to expend its resources in serving the gospel of Christ in programs and in service to the world in order for its members' giving to increase.

Some people who have worked with the finances of our local congregation often ask, "How did we become such a generous church?" They remember when we could not make a one-hundred-thousand-dollar budget. Our local church budget has increased by more than three and a half times what it was ten years ago, and we have built a new facility on a new site at a cost that would have seemed incomprehensible in previous years. We are experiencing rapid growth with delight and amazement; however, growth is not the most important thing in the difference between then and now. Prayer groups; increased mission spending; catching and casting a vision of the church becoming a regional teaching church; increased ministry with children; and a growing friendliness and willingness to become a more inclusive congregation racially, culturally, and socially have all made the real difference. A strong focus on the primacy of Scripture in a measured and balanced way that holds onto the discipline of tradition and history is central. Also a willingness on the part of the congregation to step out and involve itself in shaping the community in a time when the city and county are pliable helps people find the spiritual sensitivity and the challenge that springs money loose.

People want to give to something seeking to be born and living, not to maintaining what is and what has not worked in the past. When a congregation stops living in the spirit of seeing how little it can do and begins to ask how much it can do for Christ, money flows more freely. The members of the old mainline churches by and large are a little more prosperous than are the members of other traditions. These Lazarus-potential churches can be raised to new levels of ministry. Instead of crying about how bad it is, we must celebrate how good it can be and live toward these positive possibilities. We must dream dreams and see visions and then work with the accountability of hired laborers to make the dreams into substantive reality. Lazarus churches have to believe in what can be and seek that with passion and power.

We must propagate the potentialities instead of grieving over the death or dying of the church. Ministry is well received when lovingly given in a Jesus-shaped expression of care and concern. To tap into positive potentialities with fruitful witness and service, the Lazarus church must know the power from above. The risen Jesus asked His disciples to wait for power from above, and then they would be His witnesses to the world.

PLANT THE POWER

The Holy Spirit power from above inspired the disciples of Jesus to witness to the life, ministry, death, resurrection, and ascension/exaltation of Jesus and what this could mean for human life. Pentecost, the day the church was birthed, reveals the Holy Spirit's chief function to gift, empower, and sustain disciples of Jesus in witness to Him as the revealed love and truth of God that saves individuals so that they might fully live (see Acts 2).

The Holy Spirit is not the message of the church—Jesus Christ is the message, the gospel. I remember several years ago when a woman so enamored with her recent experience of the Holy Spirit told me she never thought anymore about God the Father or Jesus the Savior. She said now she just thought of the Holy Spirit. Who was the Holy Spirit witnessing to in her life? Sometimes congregations become victims of this fallacy. The Holy Spirit not only has the purpose of witnessing to Jesus, but that of reproducing the embodied life of Jesus as the church—the tangible, visible, active body of Christ in the world.

The Spirit always seeks body. In the beginning the active Spirit of God the Creator sought manifestation in body—thus the creation. Spirit seeking body went on to create the covenant community of Israel to be a light and witness to the nations. The Spirit seeking body was manifest in birthing and sustaining the church for Christ's purposes. The Holy Spirit seeks body and expression in Lazarus—the Lazarus church. It is here the Spirit of life wants vital expression and this Spirit desire is the power that can call Lazarus churches out of the cave into the light and then release them in power to witness wonderfully to Jesus Christ.

The power we seek is the Holy Spirit, the risen Spirit of Christ, who brings us the fullness of God in experienced faith and life, not just in thought and theology. The implanting of the power of the church is the arrival of Jesus into the soul of the church, the hearts of its people. This is the revelation of the heart of God to the world—it is the giving again of God's love to the world through the life of the church. This is the one power that can inspire, encourage, and unbind a living church in the world.

Lazarus churches are enlivened
when the power of God's love in Jesus
is born by the "near and now" experience
of the Holy Spirit.

The great function of the Holy Spirit is to plant Jesus in the church as its heart and to impart the life-transforming love of God revealed in Jesus to human hearts. Every "body" needs a healthy heart in order to freely and fully live. The church needs the heart of God given in love in Jesus Christ. Our call today is to plant this power in our churches. Lazarus churches are enlivened when the power of God's love in Jesus is born by the "near and now" experience of the Holy Spirit. This gift is not the exclusive treasure of any church or any group of churches. Lazarus churches of the mainline type are fully capable of holding within them the power planted from above.

The Christian movement is always one generation away from extinction—if any one generation is not reached, it all collapses. These old mainline churches have been vital to keeping the chain unbroken. I believe God is not through with these churches. I believe God still has a place for them in the kingdom, that new winds of life are blowing all through these congregations. Such individual congregations will be the transforming power of their denominations, the voices that say, "Roll back the stone. Lazarus, come out. Unbind Lazarus and let him go."

The challenges are many for the old mainline churches—as for all churches. However, I believe in what they are and in what they can achieve in today's world. Our world needs roots and abiding realities, something proven and true that witnesses to a God who is the same yesterday, today, and tomorrow.

Our country is challenged today in ways that are new and frightening. Since the attack of terrorists that stole so many innocent lives and brought down the towers of the World Trade Center and tore open the fortress of our security, the Pentagon, we Americans have rallied. I think of our president's words that he took from a common citizen who became a hero, "Let's roll!" I find myself wanting to say to the old churches, "Let's roll! The victory is ours!"

Chapter Six

A WORLDLY PASSION

GOD'S SAVING WORK IN JESUS IS NOT JUST about us—it's about the world. In the story of Lazarus we discover the truth that Lazarus's return to life was about more than just Lazarus—it was about Jesus, God's greater purpose.

Jesus took time away in prayer because so many who had come to visit with Mary and Martha saw His miracle of raising Lazarus. Their demands upon Him necessitated time apart with God. The Sanhedrin, led by Caiaphas, plotted to have Jesus killed because so many people were turning to follow Him. They believed in Jesus because of Lazarus, whose salvation was serving a purpose greater than his own life. The raising of Lazarus had become a sign that God had come near in power through Jesus Christ to deliver people by grace from sin and death. Six days before Passover, the people who had begun the ritual preparation for celebrating the feast wondered if Jesus would come to the banquet. Here is a witness to the larger story of God's saving purposes in history, of which Lazarus himself will be a sign of its continuance.

Lazarus's resurrection is tied to the liberating power of God in history that delivered Israel from Egypt and formed the people into a covenant community serving as the agency of God's Law and grace to be a light to the nations. Lazarus back from the darkness of death is witness to God's greater purposes for the salvation of the world.

Passover was one of the three great festivals during which every adult male Jew was required to visit the temple in Jerusalem. In this festival and its great meal of Passover, the people would recall how the death angel passed over the houses of the Hebrew people the night that the firstborn of Egypt died. They were commanded to retreat into their homes in the land of slavery and to put blood on the doorposts. Every family was to kill and eat the Passover lamb so their families would be spared death and be delivered from slavery. They obeyed and were delivered, but even this deliverance was about more than their lives. It was about going into the wilderness, becoming a people of the Law of God, and setting a whole people toward the

Promised Land and the unfolding drama of God's salvation in the world. From these people would come the rich traditions of the law and the prophets, and from them Jesus Himself would descend. God's promise to Abraham that he was blessed to be a blessing and that from him many people would descend was unfolding.

This is one story of great magnitude in God's rule of grace. It is always about more than the person or persons—it is about the whole world, about eternity. Although the old stories are set in time and space, they are filled with transcendent truth that touches eternity itself. We must see the magnificent scope of the grace and truth of God that seeks to claim our lives. In this grand picture of God's plan sits the story of Lazarus and of the Lazarus churches. Lazarus is the witness at the Passover season that God is still working and is still powerful to deliver from death, slavery, and fear.

The people looked for Jesus—would he come to Passover? They wanted to see Him and hear Him and be touched by Him. (Others wanted to be rid of Him.) Jesus returned to Bethany six days before Passover, and Mary and Martha prepared a great meal, a party of sorts. Neighbors, friends, and family gathered, and they marveled that Lazarus was at the table with Jesus and the others. He was the living sign of the active and prevailing power of God's grace. God was not long ago or far away or yet to be.

God was active in Jesus with a powerful saving grace of life. Oh, what a happy day it was in Bethany!

Lazarus's presence is a powerful witness to God's salvation purposes in history. It is a scene in God's work in the world to save the world. The Lazarus church and its members experience and claim God's saving act in Jesus not just for the church and themselves—they also participate in God's larger purposes in their own saving hope. The Lazarus church raised, delivered, and let loose upon the world is called to be a witness to the glory of the Lord and to the unfolding salvation story of God that threads its way throughout history and points to the truth of the continuing faithfulness of God to deliver from sin and death in and through its witness to Jesus Christ.

The new story of life—the Lazarus story and the Lazarus churches—provides a proclamation of the grace that God's passion revealed in Jesus is a worldly passion. The following words from Holy Scripture bear witness to this truth:

> . . . the world is mine, and all that is in it (Ps. 50:12).

> For God so loved the world that he gave his one and only Son, that whoever believes in him shall not perish but have eternal life (John 3:16).

> . . . God was reconciling the world to himself in Christ . . . (2 Cor. 5:19).

From my early childhood in the Methodist
Church I was made aware that our little country
congregation was connected to the world—that it
had a Lazarus witness to give. We had something to
do with the larger world because people called
"missionaries" came to our church and showed us
long, boring slide shows of mission-field ministries.
I didn't understand what it meant except that our
church was doing something in Africa and other
places around the world in the name of Christ. I
knew we were helping people in faraway places to
live better lives because Jesus loved them with God's
love. All this was a great deal for a church to lodge
in a small boy's heart, but I didn't know then that
these seemingly ordinary things were part of God's
salvation history. Now I know it is so, and that
elevates my little country church to Lazarus church
stature—a resurrection church—raised even in its
smallness to witness to Jesus and God's saving
purposes.

There was a time in my life when I could name all
the failures of my little childhood church, until I
began to realize that had it not been for that church I
would have no basic knowledge of the faith. It was
small and it declined once to the point of having only
eight to twelve people on an average Sunday
morning. But it told the story of Jesus. The retelling of
the Jesus story so that grace touches people's hearts is
an act of God in little old country churches as well as

high-steeple churches. I know now that I am rich because of the poverty of that little church which taught me how much Jesus loved the world and me.

A DEACONESS AND HAPPY HILL

I recall with appreciation the deaconesses that made a connection with our little congregation. At the time I didn't know the conviction of love they held for the world or the deep sacrifice they made of their lives—these women were so devoted to Christ and loved the world so much that they gave up dreams of homes and families to live in singleness to serve the mission of the church more fully.

One deaconess stands out clearly in my mind—I knew her simply as "Miss Glenn." She attended our little church often. I remember her as an older woman with white hair, clean-faced, and saintly in her appearance. I knew she worked with the poor— those outside the church whose lives were lived in "desperate straits." She also worked with the small congregations of our county. She spent much time in the county seat in a neighborhood called Happy Hill.

Happy Hill was a section of the town where the poorest of the poor lived, a truly desperate place. Miss Glenn often brought people from Happy Hill, especially children, into our church for Sunday school and worship. There are many reasons for my recalling Miss Glenn and Happy Hill.

First, there is Miss Glenn and her work. She was the most saintly looking woman I ever saw as a child. She had white hair so clean and pure, and it was always combed and in place. Her face matched her hair in brightness so that there seemed to be a light glowing about her. She was modest and yet she exuded a stable and quiet strength that I never doubted. She cared a great deal for the people on Happy Hill and our little congregation, and in my memory she is yoked with everything I knew and experienced of a connectional church.

I also experienced Happy Hill directly. I visited my grandparents, my daddy's mama and daddy, over there. I knew their poverty and need. We often took them groceries and helped them because it was a difficult period in their lives. I saw and played with some of the children there, and my mother watched me carefully when we were visiting them and guided me on my behavior.

Although we lived in another community and had sufficient resources to meet our needs, I knew the demands of making ends meet from Daddy's hard work and Mama's help in managing the little we had. As the years progressed we, like everyone else, shared in the growing prosperity of America. So I was impressed that a saintly woman of the church could roll up her sleeves and carry her clean self into the dirt and despair of Happy Hill, giving its people hope for a different life.

The church should carry the holiness of the gospel and changed lives into the dirt and despair of the world in every place and age. When the church participates in God's salvation purposes for the world, its people discover the power of being a Lazarus church—raised up not to exist for its own life but to give itself to the world in service to God's saving power.

Heart connections with the Lord lead to ministry beyond the parish in places like Happy Hill. When our hearts are met with the heart of God we are connected to the suffering world around us. Places like Happy Hill, from which the cries of suffering and desperate people peal forth, beckon to the church.

GOD CALLS IN THE CRYING WORLD

The cry of the needy and hurting is the voice of God's own anguished call to the church. The sphere of the parish's call is as broad as the world and as near as the other side of the church doors and the pews within where the people bring their tears and their laughter. We are called to a worldly passion. We are called to love the world with God's love. We are called to spend our lives as Christ's life was spent to save the world.

God always has more in mind for us than our own salvation. I want to express a biblical witness to this truth by lifting some affirmations up at the risk of sounding like "proof texting." I simply want to point the church toward understanding that our passion is not just for our salvation; but that its larger meaning is found in the context of and is servant to God's mission of saving grace for all the world—and in our case, especially that part of the world available to us. This part of the world is the arena of our work serving the greater vision of the heart of God for all people. The prophet Isaiah spoke to Israel in exile, who needed the promised salvation of God, saying, "It is too small a thing for you to be my servant to restore the tribes of Jacob and bring back those of Israel I have kept. I will also make you a light for the Gentiles, that you may bring my salvation to the ends of the earth" (Isa. 49:6).

The church should carry the holiness
of the gospel and changed lives
into the dirt and despair of the world
in every place and age.

Jesus set God's mission of personal salvation in the context of God's love for the world. When Nicodemus came to Jesus in the night and sought what he suspected resided in Jesus, he was confronted with God's personal love and worldly passion. Telling Nicodemus about the potential and possibility of salvation, Jesus said, "For God so loved the world that he gave his one and only Son, that whoever believes in him shall not perish but have eternal life" (John 3:16).

When Jesus commissioned His disciples to ministry He set dancing in their heads visions of the whole world as the realm of that ministry. "The Great Commission," the church's marching orders, includes all the nations: "All authority in heaven and on earth has been given to me. Therefore go and make disciples of all nations, baptizing them in the name of the Father and of the Son and of the Holy Spirit, and teaching them to obey everything I have commanded you" (Matt. 28:18–20).

The outline for the Book of Acts is listed creatively in the first chapter of that book. The writer gives us the purpose and structure of the book by relating Jesus' words to His disciples just before His ascension to God. He said, "But you will receive power when the Holy Spirit comes on you; and you will be my witnesses in Jerusalem, and in all Judea and Samaria, and to the ends of the earth" (Acts 1:8).

The rest of the Book of Acts is about how the gospel is offered to people in all kinds of places and in all sorts of conditions. This ministry of witness spreads out from Jerusalem to all Judea, to Samaria, and finally to Rome, the hub of the world. From Rome, highways ran outward like spokes in a wheel, penetrating the whole known world. Discipleship for Jesus' followers meant more than their salvation—it also meant that their lives were to be spent in reaching out to the whole world with God's love. Lazarus's greater purpose in Bethany and at the table with Jesus was a witness that indeed transcended his time, testifying to all the ages to come that Jesus is the Resurrection and the Life, and that God's saving work penetrates our world with everlasting hope. God calls us in the Lazarus church to a ministry of love that liberates people into full life.

THE ALDERSGATE AND WORLD LINKAGE

John Wesley revealed in his ministry what we always need to learn in the church—that we cannot have a heart for God without finding a heart for the world. After his heartwarming experience at Aldersgate, which some have called his awakening, Wesley found himself preaching in the streets and in the fields through which the coal miners passed to and from work in the mines. During his entire disciplined life of faith as an adult, from the time of his days at Oxford, Wesley had a heart for people in dire circumstances. He visited prisons. He sought to provide ministry for the poor and needy. Finally, he was shut out of the parishes. Perhaps Wesley's experience is a warning of how the church is always in danger of rejecting God's outreaching love for others. This rejection weakens the church's witness and misses many opportunities for receiving God's heart.

Wesley was not given a place to serve or preach. His experiences of God's grace active outside the churches and the resistance of the churches to his witness and ministry ended up giving Wesley a larger picture of the fields of Christian service without which there would be no Methodism today.

When John and Charles Wesley asked the bishop of London and other authorities for an appointment to a parish in the Anglican Church, they were denied. It seemed to these brothers that there would never be any likelihood of an appointment for either. They were told that the church and its authorities had a right to silence them, but they would not be silenced because they heard God's call to the world. In response to such circumstances, John Wesley wrote:

> On scriptural grounds I do not think it hard to justify what I am doing. God, in Scripture, commands me, according to my power, to instruct the ignorant, reform the wicked, and confirm the virtuous. Man forbids me to do this in another's parish, that is, in effect, not to do it at all, seeing I have no parish of my own, nor probably ever shall. Whom, then, shall I fear—God or man? If it be just to obey man rather than God, judge ye. I look upon all the world as my parish; thus far, I mean, that in whatever part of it I am, I judge it meet, right, and my bounden duty, to declare unto all that are willing to hear, the glad tidings of salvation.[9]

John Wesley was a Lazarus kind of man. His experience of God's grace in Jesus was meant to empower him to serve the world, not to enjoy only for himself and sink into snobbish self-righteousness or spiritual superiority. Saving grace in his life was grace to serve the world. Like its parent, early American Methodism had a worldly passion. It had a heart for the world and saw its mission to be the spreading of "Scriptural holiness" and the reformation of the continent.

The heart of God incarnate in the church holds up to the church the world which God loves—whose salvation God has always sought. Our personal salvation and the inspiration of the church find their source in the passion of Christ, God's love offered in Jesus' death and resurrection for the life of the world. This heart truth is the power of the church as its seeks to make itself an offering of God for the world. As the body of Christ, the church is sustained in strength when its heart is the heart of God for the world. The Lazarus church is called to this worldly passion.

In order to fulfill this worldly passion, the local parish and its denominational connections must believe that the world is worth saving. The Lazarus church has to love the people of the world. It must have the love for the world shown in Jesus' love for Lazarus when He knelt weeping beside Lazarus's tomb.

God did not call the church into existence to condemn and judge the world—the church in its parish expression must be all that Jesus was in the world, and capture in its ministry the value God places on the lives of all the people of the world. Human beings are judged by God to be worth the life of the Son of God. Jesus is not our older brother being punished for our sins so that we might not be punished—Jesus is the life of God offered for us. Jesus is God taking upon God's own self our sins, not just that we might be forgiven, but that we might also have our hearts so won by God's love that we would be free from sin and alive to God.

At the core of this incarnation truth is God's estimate of our worth and the worth of the world. This incredible worth is like a mother who holds for the first time her newborn child—one who was conceived when her heart was bound in love to another. In that moment when a new mother meets her precious child, she realizes she has offered her life to nurture and keep that child so that it might live. What a mother feels and fears for her child in that moment is what God feels for all human beings, for the world, for you and for me—eternally. If we can tap into that love power in the life of the church we may begin to see each strange, desperate, and troublesome person as a treasure held precious to God. We may be able to feel some passion for their salvation.

Salvation here is more than what we sometimes think of as getting people converted and made members of somebody's church. It ought to be so much more. Salvation means people knowing they belong to God—that they are valued, sought, and helped by the agencies of divine affection, and that every need of theirs is a known concern of our heavenly Father. They cannot know this if the church is not the leavening of such love in the flat and tasteless bread of their lives.

LOVE AS GRIEF

In every way the world is our parish. We are called to reach out to every needy person we can touch—the drug addict, the prisoner, the sexually distressed and abused, the homeless and the hungry, the war-torn children—all these sing a haunting requiem in strained notes. In the midst of their choruses they listen for different music, filled with loving-kindness, that will lift them up to a lasting hope. We cannot give them this hope if we do not perceive that they, like each of us, are made "a little lower than heavenly beings" and crowned "with glory and honor" (Ps. 8:5).

This treasure is held in broken and distorted lives—in the lives of saints and sinners. We cannot attain that "heart love" necessary to seek the salvation of the world unless we believe in the sanctity of every human life among us from the least and the best, or the unborn and the mistakenly born, or the most despicable among us, to the living and the dead—the buried and the resurrected.

Sometimes this belief in the sanctity of human life may be expressed only as grief for what could have been, since people hold within them the image of God that somehow has been distorted. Grace becomes deep agony because of lives that are frustrations to themselves and that ultimately only bring suffering to others.

Maybe God's passion for the sanctity that is not realized in despots, tyrants, crooks, and sinners can only be eternal grief. Yet God's love still acknowledges, if only in what could be, the sacred value of each of these lives. All these are sought by God's eternal love which is not restrained by the boundaries we think so ultimate in our narrow minds and small hearts.

The parish can learn to think as God thinks and to love as God loves if filled with the presence of the heart of God. If God does not love each person, however bad he or she seems to be, then we cannot believe God loves everyone—or anyone. People are treasures, often lost treasures, to God just because they are, will be, or have been.

LOVE AS HOPE

Somehow in the midst of all the strange magnificence of human life there sits One who suffers, dies, rises again, and is lifted up to lift others up. This holy and passionate One does not want us to continue to be imprisoned in things as they are—circumstances that would keep us from the fullness of life. Every great human achievement in any sphere—government, medicine, education, or religion—is a gift God seeks to give for the redemption and fulfillment of human life.

The whole creation in all its bounty and beauty is an expression of this outreaching love of the heart of God for God's creation—the natural and the human world. We are called to enter into that grand and inexhaustible passion of God as the church. We believe in the inestimable value of all God's creation, especially of every human life. A worldly passion requires a belief in and a commitment to the value of the world.

A worldly passion requires of the church, or parish, a convincing belief in the saving purposes of the church. Too often it seems to me that the administrative, structural, and decision-making life of the local parish diminishes into keeping the church alive for the church's sake. Sometimes it seems mainly given to keeping the money coming in to sustain it, to keep the buildings up and in good shape, and to keep things as they have been so that our kin and kind can continue to enjoy what we have enjoyed.

An older minister who has since gone to heaven told me about a congregation he once served as pastor. He was trying to get them to move forward in some new ventures of ministry that would have required some significant changes in the life of that church. At the board meeting one of the men present said, "You just don't get it, do you preacher? We want to keep this church for our grandchildren just the way our grandparents kept it for us. We do not want anything about it to change." That pastor said to the board, "Well then there is no need for me to be here."

The truth is that when people have no passion for evangelism—for growing the kingdom of God on earth, for reaching out and expanding the family of God—then there is no reason for any of us to be here. When there is no grief for the suffering of others or desire and effort to share God's love with them, then there is no need for any of us to be in the church. When there is no desire to transform the lives of the members of the congregation into the fullness of life intended in Christ, or to nurture and sustain one another in kindness and mercy, there is no need for us to be here. When we are not driven in our gatherings to teach and learn about Jesus or to pour out our lives in worship and devotion to God, there is no reason for us to be here.

The gap that often exists between clergy and laity sometimes centers on the issue of how the church is understood and what the purposes are for the church's existence in the world. This is a terrible gap and it is real! Sometimes this gap is between clergy and clergy or between laity and laity. A vision of the church's purposes is not the property of the clergy alone. Yet too few of either "kin or kind" dabble seriously in the arena of a purposive vision or passion for the church. Clergy often have sacrificed God's call to ministry to the idea of their work being a profession or a job. The issues of ministry become position, salary, and receiving the proper recognition and respect due a "reverend." Yet that is not how we clergy began. We began with a call or a need or a passion to do something good with our lives for God, for the church, and for others. Yet, caught up in church life, where the passions of God's purposes get overshadowed by our human and institutional agendas, we can forget how we began or why.

In order to embrace and live out a worldly passion the parish must have some vision of its purposes and how it can encounter the world with these purposes. We need to reclaim and be restored regularly to some of the key passionate purposes of the church appropriate in every age. There are some biblical purposes that must be givens in a parish's worldly passion.

First, there is the worship of God. It is the biblical understanding that the chief purpose of humankind is to know, worship, and glorify God. Our worship of God corporately binds us to God and

God's will together. Worship sets the tone of everything else we do. When I served as district superintendent I felt called to make worship the first priority of our pastoral relationship as clergy and laity. Each district pastor's meeting began with worship led by the pastors, and I served Holy Communion. Then we went into another room for fellowship and business. It is amazing how this shaped the tone and direction of our meetings.

*If we as a parish do not worship well,
we are not likely to do much else well as a church.*

Today worship has become an issue of conflict. How we worship is a point of deep debate and pain in many places. My fear is that this conflict has more to do with what pleases us than with pouring out our lives in love, devotion, gratitude, and a selfless seeking of God's will in our lives. The grandest passions can be corrupted into evil. What some people call spiritual warfare is a present conflict that must be fought in our own hearts about whether our desire for worship is a seeking to honor, serve, and love God or to please our own emotional and aesthetic prejudices. Living in our time makes me notice in a new way the fact that the first act of violence in the Genesis story centered on frustrated worship (see Genesis 4). Cain slew Abel because his own worship of God was not as pleasing to him as Abel's was to Abel.

This greatest of all the church's purposes must be approached humbly and with great care. If our worship becomes about us and not about God, the church runs the risk of being sent into the land of Nod—the land of wandering aimlessly like strangers and perceived enemies of our sisters and brothers in the church itself. Worship is the power from which all our other mission expressions must flow. Consider the attention given to right worship all across the Old Testament pages and implied in the New Testament.

If we as a parish do not worship well, we are not likely to do much else well as a church. Worship begins the fulfillment of the first great commandment: "Love the Lord your God with all your heart and with all your soul and with all your mind" (Matt. 22:37). Our worship holds within it praise and thanksgiving; hymns of faith and hope; prayers of petition and intercession; acts of giving; proclamation and response; the sacraments of inclusion, renewal, and sustaining or baptism and Holy Communion. Word and sacrament are central to our understanding of God's acts of grace and our acts of devotion in worship.

The Great Commission of the risen Christ is a commandment. It also shapes the mission statement of the church to make disciples of Jesus Christ. Jesus' commissioning of the church is found in two pronouncements to the disciples before He ascended to God. Our being sent in mission is twofold: first, there is the one we think of most often in Matthew 28, "Therefore go and make disciples of all nations, baptizing them in the name of the Father and of the Son and of the Holy Spirit, and teaching them to obey everything I have commanded you" (19–20); second are Jesus' words about the church people, His disciples *being* His witnesses to the entire world, "But you will receive power when the Holy Spirit comes on you; and you will be my witnesses in Jerusalem, in all Judea and Samaria, and to the ends of the earth" (Acts 1:8). In these two passages the worldly passion of the parish is expressed in doing and being.

The disciples in Christ's mission purposes are to do the following things:

- *Go into the world for Jesus.* We are sent in Christ's mission to the world.

- *Make disciples.* We are to reproduce the life in us in others as Christian disciples.

- *Baptize people into the fullness of God in whom fullness of life is found.* We are to baptize, administer the sacrament of inclusion, in the name of the Father and of the Son and of the Holy Spirit.

- *Teach them to obey the commandments of Jesus.* This means biblical preaching and Christian education ministries and all that accompanies them.

The question of mission emerges in both texts. We cannot make disciples if we are not disciples. As disciples we are to seek and wait for the power of heavenly grace, the Holy Spirit, in order to be Jesus' witnesses in the world. This is the parish ministry of being witnesses. This means embodying in our lives and the life of the church the life and love of Jesus. It means making real the outreaching love of God in every kind of ministry we fulfill. The church, you and I, are to be this love and truth to the world.

Finally, this basic passionate purpose of the parish continues in emphasis in 1 Corinthians chapters twelve and thirteen. In chapter twelve of 1 Corinthians we are told that we who are members of the church belong to the body of Christ, and the church is to fulfill in its life what Jesus did in His life. The church and its members are to be one with Jesus and with each other so that all ministries and expressions of the church reveal the presence of the Spirit of Jesus. In this way we together are *being* something of Jesus' continuing presence in the world for its salvation. The disciples of Jesus in the church are to be the body of Christ (see 1 Cor. 12).

In 1 Corinthians chapter thirteen, we are told in what manner to be the body of Christ—we are told to live out the agape love of Jesus. We should embrace Jesus' selfless love as our mission and way of being the church.

> If I speak in the tongues of men and of angels, but have not love, I am only a resounding gong or a clanging cymbal. If I have the gift of prophecy and can fathom all mysteries and all knowledge, and if I have a faith that can move mountains, but have not love, I am nothing. If I give all I possess to the poor and surrender my body to the flames, but have not love, I gain nothing. Love is patient, love is kind. It does not envy, it does not boast, it is not proud. It is not rude, it is not self-seeking, it is not easily angered, it keeps no record of wrongs. Love does not delight in evil but rejoices with the truth. It always protects, always trusts, always hopes, always perseveres. Love never fails (1 Cor. 13:1–8).

These two chapters of Paul's letters are expressive of the mission purposes of the parish in the world.

Our passion for Christ in the church is a passion for the world as we seek to be Christ *in* the world, not because Christ cannot do this for Himself, but because Christ wants us to have the heart of God's love in our own lives. Lazarus rises to live again in order to witness to Jesus Christ and to enter as a participant in God's salvation history. This is the worldly passion of the Lazarus church.

Chapter Seven

CRUSHED GRAPES AND BROKEN BREAD

Pour out your Holy Spirit on us gathered here,
and on these gifts of bread and wine.
Make them be for us the body and blood of Christ,
that we may be for the world the body of Christ,
redeemed by his blood.[10]

THE LAZARUS CHURCH IS A GRACE-FILLED church. Lazarus church members are called to sacramental being and living—to be an offering of grace to the world. When Lazarus was raised from the dead he participated in the life of Christ, who was to be offered on the cross for the world. At the table of celebration and thanksgiving with Jesus, Lazarus is a precursor of sacramental grace. The table held an important place in the ministry of Jesus—over and over in the Gospels, Jesus is seen at table with others. He eats with publicans and sinners, with Pharisees and scribes, and He breaks bread on the mountainsides with many people. His first miracle is at a wedding feast and He even describes the kingdom of God as a great feast. Jesus keeps the festival meals of His traditions. It is at the Passover meal that he institutes what we call the Holy Communion, or the Eucharist, or the Mass, or the Lord's Supper, or the Last Supper. Jesus determined that His church should gather around a table on which broken bread would be offered and the wine of crushed grapes would be given as signs of grace and as an experience of his everlasting presence with the church.

So it's not unusual that Lazarus, who had been raised to new life, was at the table with Jesus six days before Passover. At this table Lazarus himself becomes a sacramental sign—a living witness to the divinity and power of Jesus. He is a reminder that One has come into the world who is not like any other who has ever lived and that He has brought with Him a message of truth and grace from God.

Lazarus's sick and broken life and his death had become a means of Jesus' grace and life power being made visible and real. This meant that Lazarus was a threat to the spiritual status quo, as was Jesus. Therefore, Lazarus's life was truly a life that was now one with Jesus. In John's words, "So the chief priests made plans to kill Lazarus as well, for on account of him many of the Jews were going over to Jesus and putting their faith in him" (John 12:10). Lazarus's raised life would be at risk because of the grace he had received and the grace that others were embracing to which he witnessed. Lazarus's suffering was not over. There would be other days of disease and disappointment in his life. But now it held a different meaning and glory. Because his very life was a sign of active and powerful grace, many turned to Jesus.

This is the ministry of the Lazarus church—it is to be a sacramental sign of the grace of Jesus Christ. It is to be so one with his life and offering that in its broken bread and crushed grapes, it becomes the cause of many turning to put their faith in Jesus.

The truth is that the agency of this witness in the Lazarus church is found in the lives of the people of the church—stressed out, burdened, broken, and seeking grace in their own lives. In his classic devotional book *My Utmost for His Highest,* Oswald Chambers explains how God makes our lives like crushed grapes so that we can be poured out like wine in His service. In the daily devotion for September 30, Chambers talks about a riveting pain out of which God's call comes into our lives. God causes us to finally exclaim, "Here I am, send me!" Chambers says this call has nothing to do with our sanctification but with "being made broken bread and poured-out wine."[11]

Life crushes and breaks us and pours us out in pain. God seeks to step into this suffering affliction, caused most often by just living in this world, with the life of Christ given for us not only to raise us up to life within the world's painful realities, but also to make us into sacramental expressions of the divinity and power of Jesus Christ for the salvation of the world. We who make up the Lazarus church are to be at this table with Jesus in the manner that Lazarus was with him at the table in Bethany. Lazarus was the cause of many turning to Jesus and believing in Him.

The people who form our parishes . . .
are not just resources for supplying the church
with what it needs for its ministry to the world—
they are *the world.*

The Lazarus church is called to be a "table fellowship" of believers, and the people in the pews are the means of sacramental ministry in the world. The people who form our parishes are great treasures to be cherished and nurtured. They are not just resources for supplying the church with what it needs for its ministry to the world—they *are* the world. They sit in our sanctuaries with broken hearts, worries, and fears that rob them of the fullness of life. They are sheep who need shepherding—God's call sitting right in front of us. Sometimes we abuse and use them in our rush to get out there in ministry to the world. In our attempt to save the children of the world, we lose our own children whom God has placed right in our hands.

The passion of the parish is diminished when the suffering people of the parish are treated like objects for the use of others in the parish—when their pains are ignored and their pocketbooks cherished. We must see these people as our sacred call. We are meant to minister the grace and mercy of Jesus Christ to them that their broken lives might become sacramental; then their crushed lives become grapes from which the wine of new life can be made for the refreshing of others, and their broken hearts can become the bread of God's grace that they can share with the world.

In every communion service we come to the altar praying that we might together receive the life of Christ so that we would be for the world the body of Christ. All we have to offer for this purpose is the "crushed grapes and broken bread" of the lives of the local church. It would be a shame to miss the mark and just leave them as wrecked lives—from whom we try to drain what the church needs.

SACRAMENT SITS IN THE PEWS

A young boy caught my eye one Sunday as I walked down the hallway of the church. He was there in his sport coat and matching pants, very much in style with all the others. He was about nine years old, and a little pudgy. He loved his pastor and his church. By all appearances he looked fine, but I knew that he often wept and cried for his mommy and daddy. No one in the church would ever guess that things were not right. I wondered if in time we would lose this child God had given to us, and my heart hurt.

Some parents brought another child of the church to me. They said he had some attitude and behavioral problems. It appeared to me that maybe these fine-looking parents who seemed to have it all—money, a fine home, the American dream—were experiencing a lot of confusion and pain in their own lives. Getting their child "fixed" would not begin to heal their hurts. Yet no one would guess that alcoholism was an issue in this family—perhaps not even the mother, who herself owned the problem. Very often alcoholism is not even considered by counselors when people come to them, yet it is there in all its demonic power, attacking the best, most creative, and most sensitive members we have. How could these be saved, and experience God's grace so that their lives could become grace in the world?

People fear for themselves and for their children. They fear being found out by their spouses. They don't understand what happened to their marriages for which they once had the greatest hope and sense of commitment; they aren't sure how to be single or parent their children alone.

These people enter the church doors each week and take their pews. Worship leaders tell them they ought to smile and be happy in the Lord, but I can see that they barely found the strength to get in the church door and that it took great courage to face the congregation and consider God. I admire these people—and I fear failing them.

Hurting and hoping they come to us—they are the power of the church. Passion can mount up in them and God's love can so sustain them in hope that their very sufferings become the greatest resources for ministry of the body of Christ. But they must first be loved by the church and ministered to by the heart of the church. The parish must become the hand of God that can take their lives and transform them into a means of experiencing and sharing grace.

RISKING THE CROSS

It seems to me that the church loses its pastors and spiritual leaders too easily without putting up enough fight. Saving folks always requires a cross—taking a risk and becoming vulnerable. Fear of lawsuits or embarrassment causes judicious leaders to take the easiest way out by throwing away the wounded shepherds and soldiers of the church. Sometimes we might look into our own broken lives and see what might very easily have become of us—we could in all truthfulness say, "But for the grace of

God there go I." This old saying is just another way of saying, "If my life had been different—the people in it, or my circumstances, or my physical, chemical, and biological makeup, or my emotions more frayed—I could be capable of those same things." All of us have the potential for good and evil that sometimes Providence keeps us from falling into.

We have to make hard decisions about moral and ethical issues in order to protect the lives of others. I have been part of such decision-making when I served as a district superintendent and also while serving as chair of the Board of Ordained Ministry in my conference of the United Methodist Church. Yet it seems to me that we might at times risk the cross by becoming vulnerable and accessible to these suffering and fallen ones. The manner in which we approach the broken lives of the people and leaders of the church affects the compassion quotient of the church.

ALL WE HAVE TO OFFER

As witnesses to Jesus Christ, all any of us really have to offer the world is "crushed grapes and broken bread." If any of us are anything for Christ, then it is this! The ministry of the church at its purest is sacrament. It is a means of grace upon which its members feed. This is the source power of the church for its work in the world.

We must reclaim the good news that there is a shepherd of the sheep; One who stands in with us—laity and clergy. This One carries upon His own life our sorrows and our sins, bears our grief, is scarred for us, and gives us love and life again. Without this power, the church is unable to offer vital and life-changing ministry. We cannot give to others or to the world what we have not received ourselves in the life of the parish.

Yet we hold within the church this good news that there is such a One who is our hope and our message. The character of the heart and love of God is expressed in these words uttered hundreds of years before Jesus came to give the heart of God for the hope of the world:

> Surely he took up our infirmities and carried our sorrows, yet we considered him stricken by God, smitten by him, and afflicted. But he was pierced for our transgressions, he was crushed for our iniquities; the punishment that brought us peace was upon him, and by his wounds we are healed. We all, like sheep, have gone astray, each of us has turned to his own way; and the Lord has laid on him the iniquity of us all. He was oppressed and afflicted, yet he did not open his mouth; he was led like a lamb to the slaughter, and as a sheep before her shearers is silent, so he did not open his mouth. . . . For he was cut off from the land of the living; for the transgression of my people he was

stricken. He was assigned a grave with the wicked, and with the rich in his death, though he had done no violence, nor was any deceit in his mouth (Isa. 53:4–9).

We Christians have attributed these images to Jesus and His death on the cross. It is indeed difficult to read this prophet's words without thinking of Jesus. Surely the details of Jesus' death, burial, and resurrection as understood by the church requires us to make such an association.

Jesus' passion on the cross represents for us God entering into our broken lives and being broken for us. God bears our pain and carries our grief. God forgives and frees us from sin by the power of God's love revealed in Jesus and made present in our hearts by faith. We are inspired by visions and proclamations, by sacrament and prayers, by praise and dedications, by the manifestation of Jesus to us in the body of the church. In this power we know the love that liberates the heart from despair and fills it with hope. This grace makes us whole in mind and heart even when we are broken bread.

We who know the grace that has entered our suffering find the power to suffer gracefully. Suffering gracefully is more than bearing pain with dignity—it is making our lives a graceful offering to others in their pain. It is opening our lives up to life, taking hold of the hand of Jesus so that the powers of death at work in us become expressions of love and an offering of life to the church and to the world. When we are affirmed and loved by Christ and know it, then we find a passion for living, an ardent love for life itself. In this graceful experience of life in Christ we discover the power to love and affirm life itself.

In his book *The Passion for Life*, Jurgen Moltmann writes, "Basically wounds are healed only by wounds. Not by superior power, but by his self-sacrifice does Christ bring life into view for those who suffer. The idols of power and of success do not help a person. Only a suffering God can help."[12] Our suffering lives offered into the hands of Christ for His use are the greatest gifts we can give. People are most helped by those who know firsthand their grief and sorrows and who yet have been lifted up in such pain, lived through it, and reached beyond it by the grace of God. Our broken lives, the weaknesses of the hurting parishioners—when shepherded by the love of Jesus—form a passionate power for the kingdom of grace on earth.

ESSENTIAL HOPE

Essential hope requires an open life. Lives cannot be open without being so cherished that they can risk being vulnerable. This vulnerability becomes possible when in our hearts we meet the heart of God. Open lives are redeemed lives. Moltmann reminds us:

> A closed human being no longer has any hope. Such a
> person is full of anxiety. A closed society no longer has
> any future. It kills the hope for life of those who stand
> on its periphery, and then it finally destroys itself. Hope
> is lived, and it comes alive, when we go outside
> ourselves and, in joy and pain, take part in the lives of
> others.[13]

The life of faith is filled with this strange mystery. We must become "crushed grapes and broken bread" if we in the Christian sense are going to offer bread and wine to the world.

Suffering is not an option in life—it is a definite reality. Human freedom (the power to choose and the capacity to make wrong choices), human selfishness, and a runaway survival instinct cause us to bring pain to our own lives and crash against one another. A thousand things that make up life bring suffering to every soul. Suffering seems such a damnable thing, but life is turned in its directions by what we do with suffering. It is not so much what happens to us that matters, as it is what we do with it and the attitude we take toward it.

The church must continually help people see that human suffering is not the judgment of an angry God so much as it is the gift of God in the context of freedom so necessary for life to have any meaning. We are not robots but free people whose lives are set in a free universe in which God's will is finally accomplished. In the meantime, much that is contrary to God's will goes on. In this freedom we are to seek and do God's will that the kingdom might come "on earth as it is in heaven."

It is in this suffering that we are pried open to the place and priority of God in our lives. We find that we need to allow others to approach us and that we are more ready to approach others in this vulnerable state. It is in the crushing and breaking moments that we stand most ready for answers we have never before sought. Although God does not send suffering upon us, God seeks to enter our suffering to open us up to love and life. God seeks to transform our cross into an emblem of hope and new life.

Although God does not send suffering upon us, God seeks to enter our suffering to open us up to love and life.

It is difficult sometimes for the young and successful to know the humility of seasoned believers who have been broken and crushed by many things. I have marveled at some young Christians whose children are young, whose lives are on the fast track of success, and whose new faith is shiny. They are sometimes intolerant of old believers who don't express the kind of spiritual triumphalism that captures their hearts. Their bravado of faith, judging ways, and their powerful eagerness puts people off. They do not know how to minister to those who have prayed but have not been delivered from trouble or sickness. Their bread is whole and their grapes ripening on the vine— everything is bright, and they are sure this is the way things will always be.

It does not remain this way. Times come and go, the children bring other challenges, and temptations tear at their hearts. Then they do the very thing they said they would never do—they become more like mom and dad than they ever believed they would. This is the destiny of all the bright stars of the church. It seems so tragic, but it may be most graceful, if Jesus Christ who can enter every human heart and transform every life redeems it.

GIFTS NECESSARY FOR MINISTRY

Discovering God's incarnate grace and suffering gracefully can give us and our parishes the gifts necessary for vital ministry. Suffering humbles, teaches, builds compassion, opens life, and gives life through us to the world. We are indeed called to be "crushed grapes and broken bread" for the world. May we stay at His table until the Holy Spirit is poured on us, until the gifts of bread and wine become for us the life of Jesus, and until we become in our churches the body of Christ for the world. The sacramental life of the parish offered to the world is power for life. It is passion and hope and abundance of grace.

LOLLY'S STORY

Eddie and Lolly Watson and their son and daughter were a beautiful family. They were successful. Every place they moved was blessed by their leadership and their capacity to reach out to so many people. They always found their way into a church and became vital and influential members. The children were popular in their circles of fellowship. Everything was grand and good in their lives. Then one night a phone call came—the kind of phone call that all parents of young adults fear.

Eddie answered the call. The voice on the other end gave him the sad news that Edward, his and Lolly's only son, had been killed in an automobile crash. Lolly picks up this story in her own words that follow. She shares how Edward's death crushed her, and how in the ensuing weeks and months she was opened to God and life itself in a deeper way. God's grace worked in her sorrow and pain to shape her into a more sacramental expression of God's grace than she had been before. We can all learn from her journey how we might become a part of the body of Christ given for the world. Lolly and Eddie have become true members of the Lazarus church and are genuine Lazarus people.

On July 18, 1999, my husband, Eddie, and I received the phone call that every parent lives in fear of receiving. Hearing only one end of the conversation and the heartache in Eddie's voice, I knew immediately that we had lost Edward, our precious, passionate, twenty-one-year-old son. As my body sank into a shock that would carry it through the hospital and funeral home scenes, my broken heart found a peace that assured me that Edward was "finer than fine," and that he was at that very moment rejoicing in his triumphant home. My pain, however, is the pain of a mother questioning how she survives the loss of a child. When your life has revolved around your precious children and your every thought and action somehow molds them into the person they become, of what importance are those thoughts and motions when the child is no longer there? How can I survive without that bear hug? How can I survive without that quick humor? How can I survive—and do I really want to?

The last two years have been years of dark moments with shards of brilliant light to break the darkness. Since the world will not allow you to mourn forever, I returned to the motions of getting through life. However, to quote the author of Ecclesiastes, "Meaningless! meaningless! . . . utterly meaningless! Everything is meaningless" (1:2). Eddie would gently remind me that I should focus on the living; however, my thoughts and heartache remained with Edward. As

Gene Wise, an Episcopal minister, told me, "Lolly, your loss is like the loss of a finger to the hand. The hand will heal, there are other fingers, but your hand will never be the same." Well, I can attest that God is the great healer.

My adult years had been driven by the desire to be "super mom," "super wife," and businesswoman of the year. I derived my identity by conquering and excelling. There were always new territories to be conquered. Looking back, I remind myself of an expensive, elaborate vase—capable of holding flowers, but in itself taking away from the beauty of those flowers. Edward's death turned me from the expensive, elaborately adorned vase to a clay jar, worn and cracked by life. However, God has taken that clay jar and made something wonderful from it. For only now in my brokenness does God shine through. I spent forty-nine years planning my life and hoping that it was in accord with God. If not, I hoped God could adjust. And many times, I prayed that God could forgive—but I was not willing to change my actions. In other words, the giving was one-sided. Lolly was in control!

July 18, 1999, was the day that life brought me to my knees; and for the first time I stood only with the help of God. I have claimed Romans 8:28 every day since then, "And we know that in all things God works for the good of those who love him, who have been called according to his purpose." And true to his word, God has kept his promise. This mother can make nothing good come from the death of her precious son, but God has. Young people gave their lives to God the day of Edward's funeral. Countless young people who never buckled up before are doing so because of Edward's death. But the spiritual journey God has given me—the cracked clay jar, the crushed grape—is phenomenal. I begin every day with prayer. I end every day with prayer. I look to God's direction and I pray for opportunities to witness. I now teach a senior-high class at church, hoping to plant a craving for such a spiritual journey. This is an amazing change for the girl who could organize alligators into a welcoming committee. I face each day with the expectations of Lamentations 3:23, for "Great is Thy faithfulness . . . moment by moment new mercies I see. All I have needed thy hand hath provided. Great is Thy faithfulness, Lord unto me." And I proceed in the assurance that God—not Lolly—will deliver. The depression still haunts, but God sends me such beautiful messages of hope—messages that I suspect were always there, but I never took the time to see. Now I live for them!

We can learn from Lolly's story that in order to become representations of Christ to the world, we are sometimes required to face tragic realities and to take hold of the daily grind, learning to look upon Jesus as the mediator of our lives and as the means by which we can give ourselves redemptively to others. Life can become grace-filled, though painful, if we receive and give life through Jesus Christ. We are then raised up to be Lazarus people.

THROUGH CHRIST

As we gaze upon Jesus until He is so real to us that we invite His life into our lives, we recognize that we must approach our life only through His life within us. We cannot really receive or appropriate our lives except in and through the One from above who takes up residence in our hearts.

If we approach our lives directly, without seeking to know ourselves through the message of Jesus, we will experience our lives as flawed and impaired. Unless we know that we are eternally valued—although sinful and confused, suffering and strained, broken and scarred at many levels— we will either think of our lives as unworthy or become convinced of our invulnerability. Or we may begin to believe that we are more valued than others.

In Jesus we can recognize that our successes and failures do not define us—God's love does. In Jesus we can rejoice that our sins and mistakes do not define our lives—God's forgiveness and grace do. In Jesus we can approach our lives fully aware of the complete truth about ourselves. This truth frees us from despair and confusion because we hold the treasure of grace and mercy within.

The light of Jesus' tender grace guides us into the fullness of our lives. If we do not approach our lives in this graceful and truthful manner, we will be eaten up with guilt, or feel worthless, or deny our human condition by deluding ourselves into believing that we are grand and good and never in need of the strength and love of others or of God. We become earthbound.

In Jesus we can rejoice that our
sins and mistakes do not define our lives—
God's forgiveness and grace do. . . .
This truth frees us from despair and confusion
because we hold the treasure
of grace and mercy within.

On the other hand, we find hope and courage when we see our lives through Jesus' Word. Through the life of Jesus lived and experienced in the life of the church, through the outpouring of our lives in service to others, through prayer and study, through meditation, discipline and fasting, and through the power of the Holy Spirit we find enduring value. We have to walk through our hearts with Jesus to find our lives.

The life of Jesus for the world calls us to avoid approaching others thinking of what we need and want from them instead of how we can love them or give to them. Some truth, some kindness, some purpose greater and purer than the passions and powers of our own neediness and yearnings for others must filter and direct our path to others if harm is to be avoided.

Deitrich Bonhoeffer wrote a book titled *Life Together*, which grew out of his experience of deep Christian community in an "underground" seminary established by the Confessing Church during the Third Reich of Adolph Hitler. In that book Bonhoeffer reminds his readers of the need for Jesus to be the focus of our Christian approach to others. He makes two very profound statements to this effect.

First, Bonhoeffer says, ". . . the Christian is the man [woman] who no longer seeks his [her] salvation, his [her] deliverance, his [her] justification in himself [herself], but in Jesus Christ alone."[14] Because we have found salvation in Jesus, we no longer seek salvation from others. We don't need them to make us feel valued and valuable. We have a security of grace within that keeps us from having to take from others something we need to make us complete. We are now free to give to them. Taking makes way for giving. We can truly be with others in loving ways.

Second, Bonhoeffer reminds us that, ". . . a Christian comes to others only through Jesus Christ."[15] Without Christ we cannot know our sisters and brothers. Without the selfless love of Jesus we relate to others out of our neediness, ego, prejudice, claims, and demands of them. If we do not have a higher truth than our own truth to guide us, we may find ourselves trying to make others be what we think they ought to be. We try to control and shape them. We tend to be critical and condemning. We may want so much from others that they despair of ever living up to our expectations.

This is what relationships become when we approach others without any truth or transcending grace to guide us into their lives. Marriages are wrecked. Friendships are broken. Churches are torn asunder. All because we have not learned the wisdom of approaching one another through the mystery of Christ's love.

The Lazarus church must approach the world through the experienced grace and love of Jesus. If the church relates to the world from its own prejudices, lack of understanding, or even through its own theology that hides Christ from others, it will either push people away with judgment, offer a "cheap grace" that fails to address our fallenness and need of redemption, or it will be so enamored with growing in numbers that it will compromise the life of Jesus.

Today, old churches are called to be Lazarus churches. The old mainline kind are rich vessels of lasting truth and enduring grace with resurrection potential. They have a richness of history that a world awash in constant change desperately needs. Old churches broken, poured out, dying, and entombed in darkness can be called out, raised up, and let loose to serve the present age. If they sit with Jesus at His table they can be churches who turn many to faith in Jesus, and the kingdom will come!

In this witness, Lazarus churches may become so influential and effective that, like Lazarus, they will threaten the powers of death and risk their very lives. They might again find themselves opposed by the society in which they give their witness of scriptural truth and social holiness. If so, then they will know they are truly alive and walking in the suffering ways of the Lord who has raised them to new life of a different kind. Thanks be to God if this comes true. God has not given up on us, and neither should we. God has a plan, and we are part of the plan—so rejoice and be a Lazarus church!

Conclusion

THE MARKS
OF A
LAZARUS
CHURCH

THE LAST CHAPTER OF THE LAST BOOK OF THE Old Testament, the prophecy of Malachi, begins with this promise, "Surely the day is coming . . . for you who revere my name, the sun of righteousness will rise with healing in its wings. And you will go out and leap like calves released from the stall" (Mal. 4:1a,2). This promise captures the spirit of new life offered in Christ and that resides in the heart of the church's witness and life.

My mother's parents were farmers who had a small herd of milk cows. In the spring the cows would calve, and the young calves would often be put in the barn stalls. They would be kept in the barn at night and let out at sunrise when my grandparents went to feed and to milk the cows. These calves were a sight to behold—they would rush out of the stalls, their breath making gray puffs in the cold morning air. They would jump about and shake their tails as if they had just discovered life. They seemed so happy, so filled with vitality.

Imagine how Lazarus must have felt when he emerged from his tomb—how changed his vision of life was. Can we imagine how fresh the air must have been to him as he breathed it in and out? I think of another early morning when the women went to Jesus' tomb and found He was out and about. With the foggy breath of the morning, the dew on their feet, and the warm sun on their faces, they must have been grasped with a feeling of life much needed after the terrible darkness they had just experienced. How strangely hopeful life is just after sunrise and you are let loose from the perils of your own weaknesses and the night's darkness has passed. The new day is bright, and suddenly there are infinite possibilities. We could find ourselves leaping and jumping and praising God. This new day of resurrection is the heart of the church's witness and the goal of its work.

The church is a resurrection community. The worship of the Christian community does not come on the last day of the week or indicate a day of rest. The Christian community worships on the first day of the week. It is about beginnings, launching forth into the mighty oceans of God's new grace with vast opportunities available. The Lazarus church opens the door of opportunity.

A Lazarus Church is a church that holds to and affirms the core values of the historic, ecumenical, and holy universal church; that confronts its needs and the needs of the world; that is compelled by a grand vision; that communicates that vision so that it is contagious; that continues to be open to a dynamic and unfolding vision that is not static and stayed; and that is careful not to deny its own heritage.

A LAZARUS CHURCH
HAS ENDURING CORE VALUES

In the Lazarus story, Jesus himself and the family of Lazarus, however charged by a new vision of the kingdom of God, held to the core values of the ancient faith of Judaism. The central values of the Law of God, and the lifestyle inspired by the spiritual under-standing of the theology of a living God who is One and has moral and just character, who is all powerful, is active in human affairs and personal life, and who gives promises to people who are in a living covenant with God defined them and their meaning. The Messianic expectation held them in hope and for Jesus defined his life purposes. Lazarus raised to new life was a man who benefited from the core values of a living religion—the religion of Jesus and his people.

In our age and time the old churches of the mainline, if they are to become Lazarus Churches raised to new life and revitalized in mission and ministry, must embrace the core values of the ancient faith, of the early church, and the proven values of faith and grace declared in the ancient creeds and the experience of the historic, and holy ecumenical universal church. The Lazarus Church is called to declare the fullness of God as Father, Son, and Holy Spirit. The Lazarus Church is defined by

---

The Lazarus Church is called to declare the fullness of God as Father, Son, and Holy Spirit.

---

the centrality of Christ who is the Son of God, the Savior of the World, and Lord of all who holds within His person, message, life, death, resurrection and ascension the restorative powers of life eternal. The Lazarus Church must believe in and be motivated by the primacy of Scripture and be held accountable to the supremacy of God's grace made real in Jesus Christ. Its message must ring clear like a trumpet call for individuals to enter into the ranks of God's people determined to make a living difference in the world.

A Lazarus Church is clear about its core values in Jesus Christ, cherishing every human life and believing in the resurrection power of Christ available to it. It must believe love is greater than hate and that in Jesus Christ life is more powerful than the powers of death.

A LAZARUS CHURCH CONFRONTS NEEDS

In the Lazarus story Jesus is called to Bethany because Lazarus is ill. Those who loved Lazarus confronted the need and sent for the Savior. Lazarus churches do not hide their heads in the sand—they look around for what they are called to do, what they have failed to do, and what the world around them needs from the gospel message of Jesus Christ.

Too often churches see only what they want to see. The Lazarus church looks at itself through the eyes of Jesus' love for the church. What does love require of it? The question is not, "What do we want the church to be and do?" but "What does the life, death, and resurrection of Jesus call for our congregation to be and do?" How does this call claim the life of our congregation today in this place and at this time? A Lazarus church moves beyond evaluating its needs from the perspective of the desires of the people to considering the claims of Christ on their lives and on the church.

This new perspective means challenging the congregation's shortcomings. It means taking a hard look at where the unmet needs are and looking at possibilities with open minds. It means asking,

"What can we do for the Lord? How can we serve this community? How can we reach out to the world?" A Lazarus church asks the penetrating questions necessary to reshape its own life by the standards of Christ in the face of human need. The Lazarus church is not afraid to confront the needs of the church and the world, and it is not in denial about the realities of neediness.

THE LAZARUS CHURCH
CATCHES A GRAND VISION

After experiencing his release from the tomb through the power of Christ, Lazarus must have looked at the world through new eyes. How often do we look at a certain scene in our lives, at our backyard or some portion of a highway we travel often, and then one day we are in a different mood and see the place in a new way? For some reason we had never noticed a tree or a flower or even a house in that way before. Sometimes falling in love does that to people. Or something of Jesus may have touched our hearts that day, and we know that God is full of grace and mercy and kindness as well as being all-powerful and righteous. Things appear different in this kind of vision. Our problems shrink a little and life seems not only manageable, but also exciting. We begin to set goals and see how we can change things.

Possibilities replace the debilitating troubles that have haunted us.

The church is called to confront needs as such opportunities. It is to move into the challenges to its life and ministry with this kind of freedom to consider the larger dimensions of God's world and to stand in the magnificence of Christ's love. Within this grand vision the Lazarus church is called to confront *what is* with *what can be*.

It sometimes takes a renewing experience of the Lord to awaken this seeing with the eyes of our hearts. During a particularly difficult time in my ministry I was troubled both by the challenges of the congregation and the needs of my family, both of which seemed impossible to meet. Finances at home were low, and struggles were real among members of the congregation. We needed vision that transcended but addressed all these things. I was scheduled to preach a week of revival services with a minister named Henry Cortner. Henry had cancer, and these would turn out to be his last revival services as a minister. He was sick all week, but he kept up a bright smile as only he could do with his shiny bald head and glistening face. He was such a kind and gentle man, and he had quite an impact on me all week.

One night during the service it began to storm. When the electricity went off, someone placed a lighted candle on the pulpit, and I just kept on preaching. As I was describing the crucifixion of Jesus, the natural world's response was powerful thunder and lightning. The thunder outside shook the church and the bright lightning astonished us as we worshipped in the darkness. A grandfather, a son, and a grandson in the same family all came forward that night and made a profession of faith, decisions that changed their hearts and their homes. The grandmother made me a ceramic statue of Mary and Joseph and baby Jesus as a gift of gratitude for the services.

I was driving back and forth that week from my home about eighty miles away. The drive gave me plenty of time to think. One night after the services I was caught up in a reflection on the nature of God as revealed by Jesus. Then I began to be aware of an unexpected presence in the car that was as close to being a physical sensation as something can be without acutually being a physical presence. I knew I was not alone. I kept thinking about how to capture my experience in thought, and all I could think of was that I felt the presence of pure and perfect love. I was overcome with emotion—I stopped thinking, *What am I to make of this?* and instead I began asking, "What am I to do with this? What does this require of me?" All I could think of was that I must tell people that I loved them.

When I got home I told my wife that I loved her before she could hardly get the door open. I told my children I loved them. I called my parents the next morning and told them the same thing. Somehow this experience of infinite grace enlarged my vision of life—old problems became new opportunities. I had renewed energy and saw things differently. My problems didn't go away, but I did stop delaying my need to deal with them. They were met in a different context.

It is from such a grace-filled place that the Lazarus church is called to confront its needs. From this powerful perspective the church has a grander expectation of itself. It is energized, seizing opportunities that before it might have overlooked. The Lazarus church catches a grand vision that is full of the grace and the wonder of God—and God's possibilities.

THE LAZARUS CHURCH COMMUNICATES ITS VISION CONTAGIOUSLY

Lazarus's raised life communicated the vision of Christ for the world. There was a contagious power in Lazarus's resurrection that drew people to Jesus—the miracle of the barriers of impossibility were broken down and life was liberated into a world where all good things are possible. The church must see the larger vision of how things can be through Christ. Once it begins to have a vision for its life and ministry, it must get excited about communicating that vision. It must draw upon all the resources at its disposal. The communication must be as creative as the vision is exciting—the more creative the church gets in shaping its communication of the vision, the more excited the people who are called to communicate it become. Contagion builds. Another thing that happens is that the vision becomes clearer and expands as a result of the communication so that people get caught up in a new energy and they themselves begin to grow and expand the vision.

All along the way there will be challenges that confront the vision; however, the creative and positive energy that builds will overcome the negatives. It may take a long time, but some of these doubters will come along as the contagion grows. Others will leave. The leaders have to believe in the vision enough to pay the cost to grow the vision within the congregation.

A Lazarus church prays for God's grace to be revealed in its communication. If the leaders believe in the vision, then their communication must at every point include a witness to Jesus Christ and God's purposes. The church is about the questions, "Where is God at work and how can we join God in that work? How does this serve the purposes and ministry of Jesus Christ? How will it bless the people of God and serve the world?" This kind of communication is inherently contagious.

THE LAZARUS CHURCH STAYS OPEN
TO AN UNFOLDING AND DYNAMIC VISION

When Lazarus was raised from the dead his life must have been a constant discovery of unfolding vision. Living in such a mystery must have daily opened him to new layers of his own life's meaning. There must not have been any end to this dynamic living for the rest of his time on earth.

When God gives a congregation a vision it steps into a living, dynamic reality. There are many levels to vision—what we see holds underneath it a mystery larger than we at first realize. A Christ-inspired vision will take us many places we did not expect to go. We must buckle up and keep our lives open to the vision. We must know it is larger than we think and be courageous enough to keep our eyes open. We have entered a life zone that is dynamic, where everything becomes soft and pliable. We are caught up all at once in life forces greater than we have experienced—the vision is launched and we are committed and on our way. But it is a journey that transcends our understanding. We must live in its mystery and keep our lives open to what it will reveal. This is the adventure of a Lazarus church: it is both exciting and fearful, but it is always worth the journey. It will make more of our church and us than we ever dreamed possible.

A LAZARUS CHURCH
IS CAREFUL WITH ITS OWN TRADITION

Lazarus was raised to new life and continued to hold to the practices of his people's traditions. He is last seen at the table with Jesus in preparation for the celebration of the Passover of his faith tradition. His life was redefined within the context of his learned faith and practices.

Denominations have traditions that have held meaning for a long time that are unique to them in the Christian family. Traditions can be stale and lifeless forms. They do not have to be. They can give direction to ever new and emerging life in congregations. I have observed that congregations who get too far outside their traditions and history have a difficult time surviving in a vital way over a long period of time. Two congregations come to my mind.

One was a congregation of a mainline denomination, which for several years was led by a minister who did not really care for his church's practices and core values. For a time under his leadership the congregation thrived. However, when he left it was lost in a sea of chaos. It had no anchor or rudder to help it. It had lost its traditions and practices that could have sustained it in meaningful ministry. It did not know its own identity.

Too often—when congregations get too far from their foundations and historic experience—

they run the risk of being focused on a minister's personality and can become rather cultic. They would never think that of themselves, and the minister would be abhorred at the thought of contributing to such an expression of faith—but it happens to people who are inspired and have good intentions, but have no tradition to guide or hold them steady.

I recall a man who left the church I served as pastor to go to a new church that stood outside any particular tradition. He was excited about their spirituality and inspired worship. Several years later I was appointed to a community in which he lived. He was an elder in the church he had joined. He called me one day and asked for a meeting. When we met he said he wanted to come home. In the church where he was an elder he felt there was no tradition, that his children were not finding clearly defined Christian roots, that the hymns were lacking a strong theology and that there was no discipline in the life of the congregation. Clearly, the sustaining he needed in the life of faith called for some defined tradition of meaning and message that was proven over time. A Lazarus Church raised to new life in Christ does well if it holds to and contributes to people's lives a living tradition. It puts itself and others at risk if it gets too far beyond its own traditions.

ONE CHURCH'S JOURNEY BEGUN ANEW

First United Methodist Church of Murfreesboro, Tennessee, is an old congregation. Born in 1820 at a camp meeting at Windrow, Tennessee, the congregation moved to a new multimillion-dollar facility in 2003. This relocation is about more than a building—it is about a vision that grew out of a need.

The church facilities had grown overcrowded. Sunday school classes were meeting in two buildings other than the education space attached to the sanctuary, one of them the city art center across the street. No more room for classes could be made. Three Sunday morning worship services were held to accommodate the members. Parking was inadequate, and property could not be purchased around the existing facilities to continue growing the congregation.

At the same time the vision of the church to be involved in more hands-on mission expressions grew, and four mission trips outside the United States were conducted each year. Families with small children began to crowd the church more and more. It wasn't unusual for us to baptize two to three babies at the Sunday morning services. We took over classrooms to create five nurseries, and these were overcrowded. There was no lawn or campus for children and activities. The congregation was called upon to begin a Latino ministry, and two Latino pastors came on the staff in partnership with the Tennessee Conference Council on Ministries' commitment to Hispanic Ministry. The church began dreaming about becoming a regional teaching church. God was doing something in our lives.

When the question surfaced as to whether to remain where we were or to relocate to another site, we had no idea what to do. We were debating the issue in a Building Committee meeting when an older member who had no family and who professed faith in Christ and was baptized only within that past year came forward with a gift of twenty acres on a busy road in the heart of a growing part of the city. We decided to take the gift and propose to the congregation that we relocate and build all new facilities, including a sanctuary and education and fellowship space. This was a mighty big vision.

We wanted to go ahead and build a grand sanctuary, because we believe that the worship of God is primary to the church and the one thing that is uniquely its own. We wanted the world to know that we worship God first, believing that everything else would grow out of and be defined by worship. Worship would be the thing that powered and defined our growing vision—and indeed our worship attendance has tripled over the last eleven years.

Our leadership sought to be as creative as possible in communicating the mission and ministry vision of the church that called for a new site and a new facility. Videos, brochures, creative meetings, a strong prayer ministry, and witness to Jesus Christ were brought together with a fund-raising plan to get us started. It all clicked and succeeded by the grace of God and because it was a spiritual vision of new life for children, families, singles, and older adults.

Little did we know what was about to happen. Mr. Richard Siegel, the parishioner who gave the land, changed all of his estate plans right after his baptism. Without any of us knowing what he had done, he left the church approximately $1.3 million to be used in building new facilities. He left the city of Murfreesboro many acres of land that adjoined the church's new property for schools and a city park to be built. He left the bulk of his estate of property and its sale that equaled something in the neighborhood of $4 million to set up the Siegel Foundation for the educational and recreational needs of children and young adults. The trustees of the Siegel Foundation were to be the trustees of the First United Methodist Church. Within a year of the congregation's decision to relocate on the twenty acres he had given, Mr. Siegel died and we found out about his will.

Mr. Siegel had no children of his own, but thousands of children and young people will be blessed because of the vision God gave him in the last years of his life. People who simply sat with him in church and fellowshipped with him during the week became for Mr. Siegel the arms of Christ who welcomed him into a simple, quiet faith. Being a Lazarus himself, Richard Siegel birthed a new thing in the life of the church.

Add to this the generosity of heart and vision of a congregation willing to take a risk for Jesus, and we are now a church on a busy thoroughfare on twenty acres between a new elementary school and a new middle school. Around the corner is a new high school that will open this fall. A new city park will be opened soon that will adjoin the church's campus. None of us could have seen all of this when we first were captured by a new vision for the church, but it has unfolded and grows as we live into its dynamic power.

The whole vision has made us a praying people. It has called us to open our eyes to see God's world as a field white for harvest. When the steel was ready to be raised we wrote our names on a beam to be lifted high over the sanctuary. We chose a Bible verse to be written on the beam from Isaiah 56:7, "for my house will be called a house of prayer for all peoples." We didn't know then what we know now.

God certainly had more in mind for us than we knew when we wrote our vision statement on the steel beam. It also occurs to me that seeds for being a global church are being planted within our congregation. Here in rural Middle Tennessee we have members in our congregation from Indonesia, the former Soviet Union, Japan, China, Puerto Rico, Brazil, Mexico, Germany, Great Britain, and many other places. They are not large in number but they speak of the future that can be ours—a church in Rutherford County, Middle Tennessee—a little out-of-the-way place that is called to serve the world with Jesus' message of God's saving grace. We are called to have the heart of God for the world.

Lazarus churches must realize that their Christ is a global Christ and that they are servants of the world—indeed in some way they are all global churches.

ACKNOWLEDGMENTS

I KNOW THERE IS NOTHING THAT IS PART OF ME that has its origin with me. All things begin with God, the origin, sustaining power, and the fulfillment of all things. I have not lived in a vacuum—all that is now me, and all that is within me and that comes forth from me is a result of the responses I have made to God, to people, to places and things, to time and space, and to the reality of Christ, by the power of the Holy Spirit. If there is anything noteworthy or encouraging in this book, then others are to be thanked.

My family, including my parents White and Laura Mayo and my wife and children have provided me with encouragement and companionship during years of struggle and growing and seeking, and left me room to be myself. Patricia, my wife, has always supported me, has been very understanding, and has given space to me for free searching for God even at the sacrifice of her own space. She has been invaluable in reading and reflecting with me upon the words of the text as they have come together. Our four children have sacrificed much in order for me to serve the church.

The congregations I have served have shaped me as much as I have ever hoped to shape them. The members of the staff at First United Methodist Church, Murfreesboro, have taken responsibilities to allow me time to write and have always been encouraging of the leadership they receive from me. This gift allows room for reflection and growth. I want to recognize with appreciation the wisdom of the Staff-Parish Relations Committee of First Church for giving their senior pastor four days a quarter to get away to vision, write, and plan for the church's ministry. Much of this book and considerable expression of the vision of First United Methodist Church, Murfreesboro, has come from these days apart.

The following members and friends of the congregation have provided resources and special gifts to make this work possible. I want to thank them for grasping the larger vision of "Heart Incarnate Ministries," which is a plan for our congregation to expand its ministry by writing and publishing materials for the church in the future as it seeks to become a teaching church. They are Jim and Joyce Jackson, Martin and Jean Moseley, Wendell and Linda Mandrell, George and Nelda Pope, Tim and Brenda Menzies, and Jim and Sandy Benson.

I am especially indebted to Dr. James C. Clardy, our district superintendent, who first suggested that I write a book. Deep appreciation is expressed to Andy Miller and the staff of Providence Publishing Corporation. Andy, its president and publisher, is a friend who has encouraged and challenged me at every turn in creating this manuscript. Without him it would not have come together. I am thankful that he believes he has a call from God to publish life-changing Christian truth, and I pray this mission statement will be fulfilled in his vocation. I can hardly imagine the long hours and deep detailed work of Kelly Bainbridge, managing editor at Providence Publishing, who has edited the work and challenged me to reveal more of myself in the words I have sought to share. I thank her for all she has done.

My prayer is that I have been faithful to so many to whom I owe so much and that their passion for Christ and His church will be honored in this book.

LAZARUS REFLECTIONS AND SPIRITUAL MEDITATIONS

Chapter One
LAZARUS PRINCIPLES FOR THE CHURCH

The Lazarus story is used in the book as a metaphorical story of the church whose life is dependent upon the presence of Jesus' love and truth; of the person of Jesus as the Holy Spirit, God redemptively available to the church.

1. Jesus' love power for the church is compared to His love for Lazarus and the love of Mary and Martha for their brother.

   How do you understand Jesus' love for the church?

How does Jesus love your church?
  Denomination?
  Local congregation?

2. Describe your love for your church.

3. What does this love power reveal to you about the sacred value of your church?

Understanding the church to which we are called and which we love is important to our being agents of renewal of its life.

O God, we receive Your church as a gift of grace in our lives. Help us to value the church as a great and divine treasure given to save our souls and to make us servants of Your love for the world. Restore us to the life You intended for us, that we might become agents of renewal for the church of the Lord, in whose name we pray. Amen!

Chapter Two
HOPE FOR THE TWENTY-FIRST CENTURY CHURCH

1. Consider the membership of your church:
   Denominational membership in:
   1973_____
   1993_____
   2003_____

Local Church in:

1973_____

1993_____

2003_____

2. Consider the average Sunday morning worship attendance of your local church:

1973_____

1993_____

2003_____

3. Reflect upon the vital ministries of your church: What are they? (List)

What are the valued strengths of your congregation?

Share these in your group for discussion. What is God saying to you as you reflect upon this information?

List your prayer work that needs to be done based on these reflections.

I will pray daily at (time) _____ for my congregation and denomination.

I will pray daily for these leaders of my church.

These concerns are regularly to be on my prayer list.

O God, help us to love the church as Jesus loves it. Give us the Holy Spirit to guide us and to open our hearts to Your wisdom that we might discern Your will for the church. Give us the courage to bring Christ to the heart of our lives and to the center of the life of the church. In the name of Jesus we pray. Amen!

Chapter Three
THE DIVORCED CHURCH

In this chapter much is made of the heart divorced church. The church at Laodicea is treated as a church divorced from its heart passion.

1. What is the missing heart passion of the Laodicean congregation?

2. What is the resulting condition of a congregation divorced from its central passion and devotion?

It is often true that individuals are not in touch with their own heart—emotions, passions, convictions, and devotions.

1. Describe the life of a person who is divorced from her or his heart.

2. Compare this condition and its affect on a person's life to the same state in a local church.

Treat the church as a spiritual entity—as the body of Christ—the "Jesus life" in the world.

This chapter deals with the idea that, like the Laodicean congregation, today's churches may become victims of "accommodation unaware."

1. What is this danger?

2. How may a church move beyond this danger?

The "empty wagon" dilemma and the overwhelming power of focusing on the negative can victimize the church.

1. How would you describe the "empty wagon" danger to the church?

2. What are the sources of negativism that must be faced by your congregation?

3. What are the positive affections of the gospel of Christ that can fill the church and overcome negativism?

Eternal God, You hold all creation in Your hands. We praise Your infinite and transcending power; yet, we are thankful that You are present for us in the life of Jesus. Awaken the Christ Spirit within us, that we might know our true selves, our highest humanity, and that we might be agents of awakening the passionate heart of the congregation for Jesus Christ. It is in this good name we pray. Amen!

Chapter Four
SENT FROM THE HEART OF GOD

The focus of the church is the revealed heart of God in Jesus.

1. How do you understand the revealed heart of God in Jesus?

2. How do you understand the idea that "foxes have their holes" and the "birds their nests" but the "Son of man has no place to lay his head"? How is Jesus looking for a home in our hearts even now?

3. In what ways is it important that Jesus be the center of the church's life and witness?

4. What are the indications that your congregation is focused on the centrality of Christ?

5. How is your life a reflection of this truth?

6. How do you understand Jesus as the power of God's grace that restores the heart of the church?

Glorious and gracious God, send Your Holy Spirit upon our lives and upon the life of the church, that Christ might have His home in our fellowship. Restore the heart of the church, that as the body of Christ it might be filled with the power of Your great love for the world. Help me to be restored to Your heart, that I might have my life in You, O Savior and Friend. Amen!

Chapter Five
CHURCH UNBOUND

The church is a community of faith birthed by divine revelation. God reveals God's self to the heart of faith in creation, redemption, sustaining, and consummation. God is revealed in the community of the Holy Covenant, through prophets and priests, teachers, and holy lives faithfully lived. God reveals God's life and grace in human events and circumstances to the heart of humankind. Finally, God is revealed in Jesus Christ in whom dwelt all of God that one human life could hold. God is not discovered, but revealed. This light for the human mind and heart is essential to freedom and grace.

God frees by God's revealed grace and truth in Jesus Christ.

1. How would you characterize life lived without divine revelation?

2. How would you characterize a life lived in the light of divine revelation?

3. How is the church, the community of light and deliverance, born of divine revelation?

4. How do you understand your local congregation as a community of light and liberating power in Christ?

    Its history:

    Its present potential:

    Its place in the world of human need:

    Its future anticipated:

God's self revealed in Jesus offers the believer and his or her community of Christ the power from above; the Holy Spirit power of fellowship with God here and now, not long ago or far away or yet to come.

What is the power of the Holy Spirit?

How can this power come into your heart as a member of the fellowship of the Holy Spirit?

What was the role of the Holy Spirit in your baptism and confirmation?

How can this power be planted in the life of your congregation?

O God, Father of the Lord Jesus Christ, You have invited us to come and drink of the waters of life without price. You have promised to be a living river of life within us, ever abundant and overflowing our lives to bless others with grace. Send into our hearts the power from above and overflow us. Fill Your church with the light of Your life revealed and release Your church in power to witness to Christ and to bless the world with grace. In the name of Your revealed love, even Jesus Christ, we pray. Amen!

Chapter Six
A WORLDLY PASSION

God's saving work in us is about more than us. Christ's birthing and raising of the church is about more than the life of the church. When Lazarus was raised to new life, he became a witness to the life-giving power of Jesus; that Jesus was indeed from God and worked as the hand of God in the world. Others were coming to Jesus because of him. Lazarus was alive for the world as a witness.

1. Describe the saving work of God through Christ, by the power of the Holy Spirit in your own life.

2. How do you observe the saving work of Christ in your congregation?

3. How do you understand your own experience of Christ as a power enabling you to serve the world?

4. How is it that Jesus wants your congregation, His church, to be a servant of the world?

In this chapter it is affirmed that, "The church should carry the holiness of the gospel and changed lives into the dirt and despair of the world in every place and age."

1. How did John Wesley carry the holiness of Christ into the dirt and despair of the world?

2. How did Miss Glenn do that?

3. In what ways do you see your congregation taking the holiness of Christ into the dirt and despair of the world?

4. In what ways do you as an individual take the holiness of the gospel and a changed life into the dirt and despair of the world?

Consider planning how your congregation might do this more effectively.

If you want your congregation to do this, you must be involved in it too. Develop a plan for leading your congregation into the world, and plan your role in this work.

Loving God, on whose heart is born the searing pains of the world, we praise You for taking the sins of the world and the despair and dirt of our own lives upon Yourself on the cross of Jesus. Come again to us and raise us to new life. Empower us with Your loving heart to take upon ourselves the burdens of others that they might be raised to new life. Make the world near to us and send us the presence of Jesus with Your heart passion for the world to sustain us in serving the present age. In Jesus' loving name we pray. Amen!

Chapter Seven
CRUSHED GRAPES AND BROKEN BREAD

How is the sacrament of the Lord's Supper, the Holy Communion, or the Eucharist a means of God's grace in Christ?

What do the elements of wine and bread represent to your congregation and to you?

"The Lazarus church is a grace-filled church. Lazarus members are called to sacramental being and living—to be an offering of grace to the world."

1. What does this statement mean to you?

2. How is this description of the Lazarus church reflected in the life of your congregation and in your own life?

Broken lives restored can serve as a means of grace for the world; as signs of God's acts of love in human experience that become a light of hope to others; and as a passionate power within the restored for making their lives an offering for others.

1. How do you understand the statement "sacrament sits in the pews"?

2. How is the sacramental understanding of Christ in our suffering lives present in your own life?

Study Lolly's Story again. How did her life become more a sign of grace in her loss and grief?

Reflect upon your life's greatest pains.

1. Have you invited the crushed grapes and broken bread of Christ's own life into your life?

2. How have your sufferings been turned into a graceful offering of Christ's love to others?

Now consider your own congregation.

1. Does it honor the sacrament of the table of Christ as central to its understanding of its call to enter with its own brokenness into the world as a sign act of God's mercy and grace?

2. How does your congregation live out its sacramental life in the world?

3. Jesus has been described as "God's man for others." Is your congregation a church for others?

4. Describe how your congregation is "crushed grapes and broken bread for the world."

5. How can this become truer of your congregation—that it might be for the world the body of Christ—and of you?

Develop a plan!

O Christ, whose life was broken and poured out for us, fill us with Your passion for the suffering people of the world. Take our broken lives into Your hands and make us whole. Show us how to lead Your church into being crushed grapes and broken bread for the world. Enable us to so work with Your Word and will as to make our congregation of Your church into Your body given for the world. Make us together a true Lazarus church—restored to life to serve the present age. In Your holy name we pray. Amen!

Conclusion
THE MARKS OF A LAZARUS CHURCH

How does Malachi's image of calves released leaping from the stall capture the joy Lazarus must have felt upon release from the tomb and the grave clothes?

How does Malachi's image reflect the life of the newly restored and converted in Christ?

"A Lazarus Church confronts its needs and the needs of the world. . . ."

1. What are some of the present needs of your congregation of Christ's church that must be met if it is to more ably live the life of Christ and serve the world?

2. What things must be done to lead the congregation to meet these needs?

Your pastor is your spiritual leader and is sensitive to the needs of the church that sometimes the members do not notice, because of her or his calling and vision of the life of the whole church, not just some class or group. You may wish to invite your pastor to share her or his hopes for how the congregation can rise to the challenge of current needs as opportunities.

"A Lazarus church . . . catches a grand vision. . . ."

1. How would you describe the vision your church has for being the church of Jesus Christ in this present age and in its present place the world?

2. Does your congregation have a mission statement? If so, what is it?

3. Does your congregation have a clearly spoken vision of how to live out its mission statement? If so, how do you understand this vision?

"A Lazarus church . . . communicates its vision so that it becomes contagious. . . ."

1. How is your church's vision communicated?

2. Has the congregation caught a vision or is it held only in the minds of the few? Who is responsible for catching and communicating God's vision for your congregation?

"A Lazarus church . . . continues to be open to a dynamic and unfolding vision that is not static or fixed and that is careful not to deny its own heritage."

1. Is your congregation open to an unfolding vision; or is it fixed on an idea that is static and lifeless? "We never did it that way before."

2. How can a congregation become alive to a vision that is larger than the congregation itself so that it stands in the presence of the largeness of God and God's kingdom?

3. A congregation that gets too far from its historic traditions often gets outside of its own life to the point that it cannot sustain its vision over a long period of time and is personality driven. How is your congregation living its heritage in a dynamic vision?

Consider leading your congregation to establish a vision leadership team that is charged with discovering a dynamic vision for ministry and mission as a Lazarus church.

In what ways is your congregation called to be a "global church"?

How can this come to be vital in your vision?

God of all ages, places, and peoples, inspire in us a Jesus-shaped vision for the world. Help us to live the life of the restored. Grant us courage to imagine, to pray, and to communicate and carry out a vision that matches the grace of Jesus Christ, in whose name we pray. Amen!

NOTES

1. Michael Slaughter and Warren Bird, *Unlearning Church: Just When You Thought You Had Leadership All Figured Out* (Loveland, Colo.: Group Publishing Co., 2002).

2. Leonard Sweet, *Postmodern Pilgrims: First-Century Passion for the 21st Century World* (Nashville, Tenn.: Broadman & Holman Publishers, 2000).

3. Robert Thornton Henderson, *Blueprint 21: Presbyterians in the Post-Denominational Era* (Franklin, Tenn.: Providence House Publishers, 2000).

4. C. Peter Wagner, *Churchquake: How the New Apostolic Reformation Is Shaking Up the Church As We Know It* (Ventura, Calif.: Gospel Light, 1999).

5. Richard Kew and Roger J. White, *Toward 2015: A Church Odyssey* (Boston, Mass.: Cowley Publications, 1997), 1.

6. Albert Edward Day, *The Captivating Presence* (Nashville, Tenn.: Parthenon Press, 1971).

7. George Barna, *The Index of Leading Spiritual Indicators* (Nashville, Tenn.: W Publishing Group, 1996), 11.

8. "Near to the Heart of God." Cleland B. McAfee, 1903. From the *United Methodist Hymnal* (Nashville, Tenn.: United Methodist Publishing House, 1989), 472.

9. *The Works of John Wesley*, begun as *The Oxford Edition of the Works of John Wesley.* (Oxford: Clarenden Press, 1975–1983). Continued as *The Bicentennial Edition of the Works of John Wesley* (Nashville, Tenn.: Abingdon Press, 1984), 76.

10. "Word and Table Service II," from the *United Methodist Hymnal* (Nashville, Tenn.: United Methodist Publishing House, 1989), 14.

11. Oswald Chambers, *My Utmost for His Highest* (Uhrichsville, Ohio: Barbour Publishing, Inc., 1992), 202.

12. Jurgen Moltmann, *The Passion for Life* (Philadelphia, Penn.: Fortress Press, 1978), 25.

13. Ibid., 35.

14. Dietrich Bonhoeffer, *Life Together* (New York, N.Y.: Harper & Row, 1954), 21.

15. Ibid., 23.

BIBLIOGRAPHY

Barna, George. *The Index of Leading Spiritual Indicators*. Nashville, Tenn.: W Publishing Group, 1996.

Bonhoeffer, Dietrich. *Life Together*. New York, N.Y.: Harper & Row, 1954.

Chambers, Oswald. *My Utmost for His Highest*. Uhrichsville, Ohio: Barbour Publishing, Inc., 1992.

Day, Albert Edward. *The Captivating Presence*. Nashville, Tenn.: Parthenon Press, 1971.

Henderson, Robert Thornton. *Blueprint 21: Presbyterians in the Post-Denominational Era*. Franklin, Tenn.: Providence House Publishers, 2000.

Kew, Richard and Roger J. White. *Toward 2015: A Church Odyssey*. Boston, Mass.: Cowley Publications, 1997.

McAfee, Cleland B. "Near to the Heart of God," 1903. From the *United Methodist Hymnal*. Nashville, Tenn.: United Methodist Publishing House, 1989.

Moltmann, Jurgen. *The Passion for Life*. Philadelphia, Penn.: Fortress Press, 1978.

Slaughter, Michael and Warren Bird. *Unlearning Church: Just When You Though You Had Leadership All Figured Out*. Loveland, Colo.: Group Publishing Co., 2002.

Sweet, Leonard. *Postmodern Pilgrims: First-Century Passion for the 21st Century World*. Nashville, Tenn.: Broadman & Holman Publishers, 2000.

Wagner, C. Peter. *Churchquake: How the New Apostolic Reformation Is Shaking Up the Church As We Know It*. Ventura, Calif.: Gospel Light, 1999.

"Word and Table Service II," from the *United Methodist Hymnal*. Nashville, Tenn.: United Methodist Publishing House, 1989.

Works of John Wesley, The. Begun as *The Oxford Edition of the Works of John Wesley*. Oxford: Clarenden Press, 1975–1983. Continued as *The Bicentennial Edition of the Works of John Wesley*. Nashville, Tenn.: Abingdon Press, 1984.